About Ken Scholen's work on reverse mortgages

Rates a 10 - an ideal study book for senior citizens.

Los Angeles Times

On a scale of 1 to 10, this outstanding book rates a 12.

Chicago Tribune

An easily understood nuts-and-bolts guide to reverse mortgages.

New York Times

Enormously useful - the most detailed and comprehensive guide to reverse mortgages.

Jane Bryant Quinn

The nation's leading authority on reverse mortgages.

The Washington Post

Eye-opening - packed with rare information.

Midwest Book Review

The bible of reverse mortgages.

Guide to Retirement Living

The definitive guide to reverse mortgages.

Modern Maturity

The leading authority on reverse mortgages.

Los Angeles Times

First-Place Gold Medal, Best Book on
Financial Services for the Elderly

National Mature Media Awards

Easy to understand - you'll know what
you're doing when you finish it.

Scripps Howard News

Easily readable - the best and most
in-depth treatment of reverse mortgages.

Philadelphia Inquirer

The acknowledged national expert
of the reverse mortgages movement.

San Francisco Examiner

Detailed information on how these programs
work - advantages and disadvantages.

New York Times

Required reading for senior citizens
and their heirs.

Chicago Tribune

You won't find any better book
about reverse mortgages.

Orlando Times

Well-organized, well-presented, everything
you ever wanted to know.

Small Press Magazine

Guides homeowners through
the reverse mortgage maze.

Minneapolis Star Tribune

A valuable resource.

Consumer Reports

Contains many charts and goes
into many issues in detail.

Baltimore Sun

An outstanding book - the best book
on this topic.

Los Angeles Times

Valuable information on a topic often
only mentioned in passing in personal
finance and retirement planning books.

American Library Association

New options for savvy homeowners.

Money Book Club

Takes the mystery out of these loans.

San Francisco Examiner

The most comprehensive guide to reverse mortgages . . . the gold standard.

Kiplinger's Retirement Report

To really learn what's out there,
order Scholen's new book.

Boston Globe

Covers the pros and cons - shows how to give good consideration to a reverse mortgage.

Senior Voice

Takes the reader through the basics in easy-to-understand prose.

Long Term Care News

Written in easy-to-understand language.

Indianapolis Star

The nation's leading expert.

Bloomberg Personal

The best reference work on reverse mortgages.

St. Paul Pioneer Press

Federal Housing Commissioner's Award

U. S. Office of Housing (HUD)

Reverse Mortgages for Beginners

A Consumer Guide to Every Homeowner's Retirement Nest Egg

by Ken Scholen

NCHEC Press

National Center for
Home Equity Conversion

Apple Valley, Minnesota

First Printing 1998
Printed and bound in the United States of America

All proceeds from the sale of this book support the work of the National Center for Home Equity Conversion, an independent, not-for-profit (501-C-3) organization (see page 131).

Library of Congress Catalog Card Number: 98-065982
ISBN 0-9630119-8-7

To the 94-year-old
Miami woman who
called one day & said
"I found you through
the internet"

Table of Contents

Part ONE

Getting Started

Chapter 1

More Than a Book

Reverse mortgages have turned your home into a true retirement nest egg. This book will help you make smart decisions about that nest egg.

In Chapter 2 you will learn all the basic information you need to begin. In **Part TWO** you will see why it's important to proceed carefully. Then, in **Part THREE**, you will find out

- what's in it for you,
- where to look,
- what to ask, and
- what else to consider.

Part FOUR gives you additional resources and information for learning even more about this market. In short, this book helps you do your homework before putting your home equity to work. But it's more than a book.

A Website Companion

You may not have noticed, but you are holding more than a book. It is also a guide to a free, up-to-date "internet website" giving you a wealth of additional resources for making smart decisions about reverse mortgages.

The website will help you get the very most out of this book. And to do so you

- don't need a computer;
- don't have to know how to use a computer; and
- don't even have to ***like*** computers.

All you need is

- a friend or relative who has a computer;
- a local library with a computer; or
- a nearby senior center or any aging services agency with a computer (call 1-800-677-1116 for help).

Ask if the computer has "internet access." When you find one that does, just ask them to type in **www.reverse.org** and you'll enter an extra world of important information - at you fingertips.

If you own a computer or have "Web TV," just surf on over to **www.reverse.org** and see what awaits you. You'll find much that's in this book - plus a whole lot more.

Beginning in **Part THREE** you will see boxes like the one below - with a picture of a computer "mouse" in it. That's your signal that there are important related resources to check out on the **www.reverse.org** website.

> Whenever you see this "mouse," look for the extra information available at **www.reverse.org.**

That's why we call this book a "website companion." It tells you what you can find "online" that's new, and individually customized to your specific situation.

Don't Miss It!

Here is some of the specialized, detailed, up-to-date information you'll find at **www.reverse.org:**

- how much cash you could get this week from different reverse mortgage programs based on your specific age, home value, location, and current interest rates
- how the total costs of these loans compare
- how to qualify for specific low-cost home repair programs available in your state
- how to qualify for monthly checks from Supplemental Security Income (SSI) in your state

- a wide range of social and health services available in your area
- how much you could get for your home if you decided to sell and move
- other housing options available in your area
- help with credit problems and legal matters

There's a world of important information awaiting you on the internet. What makes it so important is

- ❑ it's a lot more detailed and there's a lot more of it than could ever fit in a book;
- ❑ it's more up-to-date than most anything that's printed on paper;
- ❑ some of it (including details on reverse mortgages) can be customized to your specific needs; and, therefore,
- ❑ it's a lot more likely to lead you to the very best decision about reverse mortgages and other options.

So give it a try. You owe it to yourself to get the very latest, most detailed, most specific and helpful information you can find. With this book – and its many internet references – you can do just that.

(And – if you ask a computer user for help – you'll be letting some internet fan do what most of them truly enjoy: introducing yet another person to the "worldwide web.")

Chapter 2

Basic Questions

A little knowledge can be a dangerous thing. So take you time with this chapter. It's got all the basic information about reverse mortgages you'll need to get started.

This chapter gives you answers to the most frequently asked questions about these new types of loans. More importantly, it answers some questions that frequently are NOT asked - but should be. So it gives you answers to questions you might not realize you need to ask.

Reverse mortgages are so different from what most people expect that it generally takes a while for the most basic information to sink in. Even experienced financial professionals are often surprised to learn

- how these loans really work
- how different their costs and benefits can be
- what you have to look out for

So take this chapter slowly – a few questions and answers at a time. Don't gulp down more than you can comfortably digest at once. Taking your time now will serve you well later on when we get into more detail.

What's a reverse mortgage?

A loan against your home that requires no repayment for as long as you live there.

How's it different?

- To qualify for most loans, the lender checks your income to see how much you can afford to pay back each month. But with a reverse mortgage, you don't have to make monthly repayments. So your income generally has nothing to do with getting the loan or the amount of the loan.
- With most home loans, if you fail to make your monthly repayments, you could lose your home. But with a reverse mortgage, you don't have any monthly repayments to make. So you can't lose your home by failing to make them.

Who can get one?

- You must own your home, and generally all of the owners must be at least 62 years old.
- Your home generally must be your "principal residence" - which means you must live in it more than half the year.
- For the federally-insured **"Home Equity Conversion Mortgage" (HECM)**, your home must be a single-family property, a 2-4 unit building, or a federally-approved condominium or planned unit development (PUD). For **Fannie Mae's "HomeKeeper"** mortgage, it must be a single family home or condominium.
- No reverse mortgage program lends on mobile homes or cooperative apartments.
- *If you have any debt against your home, you must either pay it off before getting a reverse mortgage or - this is what most borrowers do - use an immediate cash advance from the reverse mortgage to pay it off. If you don't pay off the debt beforehand, or do not qualify for a large enough immediate cash advance to do so, you cannot get a reverse mortgage.*
- Texas was the only state in which reverse mortgages were not available through the end of 1997. A statewide referendum approved them late that year, but it defined them in a way that conflicted with all current plans. So reverse mortgages still were not being offered there by March of 1998

How much cash can you get?

- The amount of cash you can get from a reverse mortgage depends on the program you select and - within each program - on your age, home, and interest rates.
- It can vary by a lot from one program to another. A typical consumer might get $30,000 more from one program than from another. But no single program works best for everyone.
- For all but the most expensive homes, the federally-insured "Home Equity Conversion Mortgage" (HECM) or Fannie Mae's "Home Keeper" mortgage generally provide the most cash. They are also the most widely available reverse mortgage programs.
- Within each program, the amount of cash you can get depends on the age(s) of the owner(s), the value (and in some cases the location) of the home, and current interest rates. In general, the most cash goes to the oldest borrowers living in the homes of greatest value at a time when interest rates are low. On the other hand, the least cash generally goes to the youngest borrowers living in the homes of lowest value at a time when interest rates are high.
- But remember, the total amount of cash you actually end up getting from a reverse mortgage will depend on how it's paid to you plus other factors.

How's it paid to you?

- That's up to you. You could take it
  - as an **immediate cash advance** at closing, that is, a lump sum of cash paid to you on the first day of the loan
  - OR as a **creditline account** that lets you take cash advances whenever you choose during the life of the loan - until you use it all up
  - OR as a **monthly cash advance**
    - for a specific number of years that you select,
    - OR for as long as you live in your home,
    - OR - if you use the loan to buy an annuity - for the rest of your life, no matter where you live
  - OR as any combination of immediate cash advance, creditline account, and monthly cash advance

- In **Part THREE** you will see how much cash you could get from the leading reverse mortgage programs.

How much total cash?

- If you take a **creditline account**, the total amount of cash you actually get will depend on two things: how much of your available creditline you use, and whether the creditline is "flat" or "growing."

- With a **flat** creditline, the amount of remaining available credit at any time only changes if you take a cash advance. Then it decreases by the amount of the advance.
- For example, if you have a flat $50,000 creditline and take out $10,000, you would have $40,000 left whenever you decided to take more.
- But with a **growing** creditline, your remaining available credit grows larger by a given rate.
- For example, if you took $10,000 from a $50,000 creditline that grows by 8% each year, and then came back for more three years later, there would then be over $50,000 left to use - because the remaining $40,000 growing at 8% for three years would become $50,388..
- So a growing creditline can give you a lot more cash over time than a flat one. That's why you need to look at more than the size of a creditline when a reverse mortgage starts. You also should consider how much available credit would be left in the future. This will also depend, of course, on how much you take out and when you take it.
- The creditline in the Home Equity Conversion Mortgage (HECM) program grows larger each month by the same rate as the one being charged on the loan balance. It keeps growing for as long as there is any credit left, that is, until you withdraw all your remaining credit.

- Fannie Mae's HomeKeeper creditline is flat. The remaining available credit does not increase.

- If you take **monthly loan advances**, the total amount of cash you actually get will depend on whether you select a plan that sends them to you for a specific number of years, or for as long as you live in your home. It will also depend how long you actually live in your home.

- If you use a reverse mortgage to buy an annuity, the total amount of cash you actually get will depend on how long you live - no matter where you live. The net value of that cash to you, however, may depend on other factors (more on this later on in this chapter).

What happens to your debt?

- It grows larger and larger as you keep getting cash advances, make no repayment, and interest is added to the amount you owe (your "loan balance").

- That's why reverse mortgage are called "rising debt, falling equity" loans. As the amount you owe (your debt) grows larger, your equity (that is, your home's value minus any debt against it) generally gets smaller.

That why it's called "reverse"?

Yes. In a "forward" mortgage (the kind you normally use to buy a home), your regular monthly repayments make your debt go down over time until you have it all paid off. Meanwhile, your equity is rising as you owe less and less, and as your property value grows (appreciates). So forward mortgages are "falling debt, rising equity" loans - just the opposite of reverse mortgages.

Here's another way to think of it. In a forward mortgage, you use debt to turn your income into equity. In a reverse mortgage, you use debt to turn your equity into income.

You are reversing the deal you used to buy your home. Then, you had income and wanted equity. Now, you have equity and want income. In both cases you use debt to turn what you have into what you want.

When do you pay it back?

- When the last surviving borrower dies, sells the home, or permanently moves away. "Permanently" generally means you have not lived in your home for 12 months in a row.
- You might also have to pay it back if you
    - ❑ fail to pay your property taxes,
    - ❑ fail to keep up your homeowner's insurance, or
    - ❑ let your home go to waste.
- But if you do, the lender may be able to make extra cash advances to cover these expenses. Just remember, reverse mortgage borrowers are still homeowners and therefore are still responsible for taxes, insurance, and upkeep.

What do you owe?

The total amount you will owe at the end of the loan (your "loan balance") equals

- all the cash advances you've received (including any used to pay loan costs)
- plus all the interest on them –
- up to the loan's "nonrecourse" limit (see the answer to the next question).

Interest rates can change based on changes in published indexes. But the more adjustable they are, the lower they start – so they give you larger cash advances. And they will be lower than less adjustable rates all during the time that index rate changes don't exceed the caps on the less adjustable rates.

What's the most you can owe?

You can never owe more than the value of the home at the time the loan is repaid. Reverse mortgages are generally "nonrecourse" loans, which means that in seeking repayment the lender does not have recourse to anything other than your home. Not your income, your other assets, or your heirs.

So even if you get monthly advances until you are aged 115, your home declines in value between now and then, and the total of monthly advances becomes greater than your home's value - you can still never owe more than the value of your home. If you or your heirs sell your home in order to pay off the loan, the debt is generally limited by the net proceeds from the sale of your home.

How do you pay it?

- If you sell and move, you would most likely pay back the loan from the money you get from selling your home. But you could pay it back from other funds if you had them.
- If the loan ends due to the death of the last surviving borrower, the loan must be repaid before the home's title can be transferred to the borrower's heirs.
- The heirs could repay the loan by selling the home, using other funds from the borrower's estate or their own funds, or by taking out a new forward mortgage against the home.

What's left?

Not all reverse mortgage borrowers end up living in their homes for the rest of their lives. Some who expect to remain living there change their minds. Others face later health problems that require a move.

So it makes sense to plan for the possibility that you may sell and move some day. How much equity would be left if you did?

- ❑ If, at the end of the loan, your loan balance is less than the value of your home (or your net sale proceeds if you sell), then you or your heirs get to keep the difference. The lender does not "get" the house. The lender gets paid the amount you owe, and you or your heirs keep the rest.

- IMPORTANT: If you take the loan as a creditline account, be sure to withdraw all remaining available credit before the loan ends. You will have the money sooner that way, and it could be more than otherwise might be left. For example, a growing creditline could become greater than the leftover equity in some cases.
- If you have purchased an annuity and then sell your home, you could continue receiving monthly annuity advances for the rest of your life. If the loan ends due to the death of the last surviving borrower, and if the annuity purchased by the borrower includes a death benefit or "period certain" payments, then the annuity's beneficiaries would receive additional cash.

What's the out-of-pocket cost?

The out-of-pocket cash cost to you is most often limited to an application fee that covers a property appraisal (to see how much your home is worth) and a minimal credit check (to see if you are delinquent on any federally-insured loans).

Most of the other costs can be "financed" with the loan. This means that you can use reverse mortgage funds advanced to you at closing to pay the costs due at that time, and later advances to pay any ongoing costs. The advances are added to your loan balance, and become part of what you owe - and pay interest on.

If a lender charges an origination fee that is greater than the amount that can be financed with the loan, you have to pay the difference in cash at closing.

What are the other costs?

- The specific cost items vary from one program to another. Many of them are of the same type found on "forward" mortgages: interest charges, origination fees, and whatever third-party closing costs (title search and insurance, surveys, inspections, recording fees, mortgage taxes) are required in your area.
- Other types of costs can be more exotic, and unique to reverse mortgages: monthly servicing fees, "equity-sharing" fees, "shared appreciation" fees, "maturity" fees.
- Although total loan costs between the HECM and HomeKeeper programs can vary enormously, many of the individual cost items within each program do not vary from one lender to another.
- Within each program, the costs that may be different from one lender to another are generally the **origination** fee and the **servicing** fee. So if you've decided on either HECM or HomeKeeper, and you want to get the best deal, these are the specific fees to compare.
- The largest total cost differences you will find are the ones between different programs, for example, between the HECM and HomeKeeper programs.

- But it is virtually impossible to evaluate or compare the true, total cost of reverse mortgages unless you consider their Total Annual Loan Cost (TALC) rates.

What's the total cost?

Federal Truth-in-Lending law requires reverse mortgage lenders to disclose the projected annual average cost of these loans in a way that includes all the costs and benefits, and also takes into account the nonrecourse limits.

This Total Annual Loan Cost (TALC) disclosure shows you what the single all-inclusive interest rate would be if the lender could only charge interest and not charge any other fees.

Specifically, it tells you the annual average rate that would produce the total amount owed at various future points if only that rate were charged on all the cash advances you get that are not used to pay loan costs. In other words, it shows you what you are paying in total for the money you get to spend.

How does the total cost vary?

On any given loan, TALC rates depend on two major factors: time and appreciation.

- TALC rates are generally greatest in the early years of the loan and decrease over time, for two reasons 1) the initial fees and costs become a smaller part of the total amount owed, and 2) the likelihood increases that the rising loan balance will catch up to - and then be limited by - the nonrecourse limit. (A major exception to this general rule is the "cost bubble" created by Fannie Mae's "equity-sharing" fee on HomeKeeper loans, which you'll learn about in Chapter 4.)

- TALC rates also depend on changes in a home's value over time. The less appreciation, the greater the likelihood will be that a rising loan balance will catch up to - and then be limited - by the home's value. On the other hand, when a home appreciates at a robust rate, the loan balance may never catch up to (and be limited by) it.

What's that mean?

If you end up living in your home well past your life expectancy or your home appreciates at a low rate, you might get a true bargain.

But if you die, sell, or move within just a few years or your home appreciates a lot, the true cost could be very high.

There's no way of avoiding this fundamental risk. You just have to understand it in general, assess the potential range of TALC rates on a specific loan, and decide if it's worth the benefits you expect you'll get from the loan.

Just remember, TALC rates are not really comparable to the rates quoted on "forward" mortgages because

- TALC rates include all the costs
- reverse mortgages require no monthly repayments
- reverse mortgages can provide an open-ended monthly income guarantee, or a guaranteed creditline (which may grow larger)
- you can never owe more than your home is worth, even if its net value is less than what your loan balance would otherwise have been.

But if you are considering a creditline, you need to know that official TALC disclosures do not account for the added value of growing creditlines. If you are a couple, you need to know that official TALC disclosures are all based on the life expectancy of single owners. But there is computer software that can show you total cost rates that correct these shortcomings. (More on this in **Part THREE**.)

One more key point: lenders currently don't have to show you TALC rates on a loan until after you apply for it. So if you want to see and compare true, total costs before you apply, you need to deal with lenders and counselors with computer software that shows you all your choices - including TALC rate comparisons. (More on this in **Part THREE**, too.)

What about public benefits?

Social Security and Medicare benefits are not affected by reverse mortgages. But Supplemental Security Income (SSI) and Medicaid are different.

In general, SSI, Medicaid, and many other public benefit programs count loan advances differently than annuity advances.

- **Loan advances** generally do not affect your benefits if you spend them during the calendar month in which you get them. But if you keep an advance past the end of the calendar month (in a checking or savings account, for example), then it will count as a "liquid asset." If your total liquid assets at the end of any month are greater than $2,000 for a single person or $3,000 for a couple, you could lose your eligibility.
- **Annuity advances** reduce SSI benefits dollar-for-dollar, and can make you ineligible for Medicaid. So if you are considering an annuity, and if you are now receiving - or expect someday you may qualify for - SSI or Medicaid, check with the SSI, Medicaid, and other program offices in your community. Get specific details on how annuity income would affect these benefits.

What about taxes?

An American Bar Association guide to reverse mortgages advises that generally

- the IRS does not consider loan advances to be income;
- annuity advances may be partially taxable; and
- interest charged is not deductible until it is actually paid, that is, at the end of the loan.

Part TWO

Being Careful

Chapter 3

Major Differences

Reverse mortgages give you a new retirement finance option that previous generations of home-owners did not have. These loans can provide an important new source of retirement cash - without requiring you to leave your home or to make loan payments for as long as you live there.

But you've got to proceed carefully, because what you don't know about reverse mortgages CAN hurt you.

Essential Facts

The most important – and perhaps surprising - facts you need to understand are these:

- You may get a lot more cash from one reverse mortgage program than from another.
- The true cost of one program may be a lot greater then the cost of another.
- A program giving you a lot more cash may also cost a lot less than any other.
- Some reverse mortgage lenders do not even offer the program most likely to provide the most cash at the lowest cost.
- To find the program that works best for you, you have to take into account
    - ❑ how much total cash would be available to you in growing versus flat creditlines, and
    - ❑ the comparative Total Annual Loan Cost (TALC) rates on competing loans.
- Many lenders do not have the computer software that can show you this information.
- Some lenders offering a variety of plans may try to sell you one plan versus another because they make more money on it.
- The TALC disclosures currently required by Truth-in-Lending laws do not fully reveal the complete pattern of costs for all reverse mortgages.

Major Choices

Which reverse mortgage plan – if any – would work the best for you?

- The federally-insured Home Equity Conversion Mortgage (HECM) is most likely to provide a lot more cash at a lot lower cost, especially if you want a creditline, or if you own your home jointly with a spouse or other person.
- But Fannie Mae's "HomeKeeper" plan may provide more cash and in some cases cost less, especially if you want a monthly advance only, or if your home is worth more than the median home value in your county.
- If your home is worth a lot more than the median value, then a private proprietary plan might work the best for you.

At the end of this chapter you will find more details on the importance of considering all your options. And **Part THREE** will give you even more detailed information. But most of this chapter focuses on comparing creditlines - because most consumers prefer them, and they present unique product comparison issues. So take a close look.

Comparing Creditlines

Table 1 compares HECM with HomeKeeper for a 75-year-old single female living in a $150,000 home in Kane County, Illinois who selects a creditline.

At closing, HECM's $77,900 creditline is $25,200 greater than one HomeKeeper option and the same as the other. But the HECM creditline grows larger by an initial annual rate of 7.5%, so it could easily provide double the remaining available cash at this borrower's approximate life expectancy 12 years later.

Yet HECM always costs less in this table. At one point (two years plus one day after loan closing), HomeKeeper's cost is double HECM's cost. This disparity is never seen by most consumers, however, because it occurs in a way that eludes Truth-in-Lending disclosure (more on this in Chapter 4).

Table 1: 75-Year-Old Single Borrower in a $150,000 Home in Kane Co., IL (11/97)

	HECM	**HomeKeeper**	
		standard cost option	equity fee option
Initial Creditline	$77,200	$52,700	$77,200
Annual Growth (initial rate)	7.5%	0%	0%
Creditline Left (1/2 spent at closing) after 6 years	$59,500	$26,340	$38,600
12 years	$91,700	$26,340	$38,600
Total Cost Rate after			
2 years	17.3%	23.0%	18.8%
2 years + 1 day	**17.3%**	23.0%	**35.4%**
6 years	11.2%	14.3%	16.9%
12 years	9.6%	12.1%	12.8%

HomeKeeper's "equity fee" option gives you more cash if you select it. But it may add a substantial additional fee to your loan costs - up to 10% of the home's value at the end of the loan. More on this in Chapter 4, too.

Differences Greater for Couples

HECM's cost/benefit advantage in this example is even greater for couples. **Table 2** shows that HECM benefits and costs for a 75-year-old couple are the same as for a single 75-year-old. But HomeKeeper couple benefits are less and costs are greater than they are for a single 75-year-old.

Table 2: 75-Year-Old Couple in a $150,000 Home in Kane Co., IL (11/97)

	HECM	**HomeKeeper** standard	**HomeKeeper** equity fee
Initial Creditline	$77,200	$40,900	$55,200
Annual Growth (initial rate)	7.5%	0%	0%
Creditline Left (1/2 spent at closing) after 6 years	$59,500	$20,450	$27,600
12 years	$91,700	$20,450	$27,600
Total Cost Rate after 2 years	17.3%	26.7%	22.4%
2 years + 1 day	17.3%	26.7%	44.4%
6 years	11.2%	15.6%	19.4%
12 years	9.6%	12.7%	13.9%

More Examples

Table 3 compares HECM with HomeKeeper for an 80-year-old single female living in a $120,000 home in Mohave County, Arizona (where the median home value is about $120,650) who selects a creditline.

- At loan closing, HECM's creditline is $20,000 greater than one HomeKeeper option and roughly the same the same as the other.
- But the HECM creditline ***grows larger*** – initially by 7.21% per year. So it provides more available cash than HomeKeeper's "flat" creditline.
- For example, if this borrower were to take $10,000 at closing and another $5,000 at the end of the next 12 years (her life expectancy from closing is about 9 years), she would retain significantly more available cash from HECM than from either HomeKeeper option.
- Yet HECM always costs less than HomeKeeper in this table as measured by the Total Annual Loan Cost (TALC) method required by federal Truth-in-Lending law.
- At one point (2 years + 1 day), HomeKeeper's cost is nearly ***double*** HECM's cost. This disparity is never seen by most consumers, however, because it occurs one day after the required 2-year TALC disclosure period. (More on this in Chapter 4.)

Table 3: 80-Year-Old Single Female in $120,000 Home in Arizona (2/98)

	HECM	**HomeKeeper** standard cost option	**HomeKeeper** equity fee option
Initial Creditline (at closing)	$71,652	$51,509	$71,696
Annual Growth (initial rate)	7.21%	0%	0%
Creditline Left (assuming $10,000 is taken at closing and another $5,000 per year for the next 12 years) after 3 years	$59,859	$26,509	$46,696
6 years	$57,651	$11,509	$31,696
9 years	***$54,930***	***-0-***	***$16,696***
12 years	$51,577	-0-	$1,696
Total Cost Rate after			
2 years	16.6%	21.0%	17.8%
2 years + 1 day	***16.6%***	***21.0%***	***32.3%***
9 years	9.8%	12.4%	13.6%

As you saw in Table 2, HECM's cost/benefit advantage over HomeKeeper can be even greater for couples than for singles. Table 4 provides another example for a younger couple in a more expensive home.

Table 4 shows that a 70-year-old couple living in a $300,000 home in Fairfield Co., Connecticut could get an initial HECM creditline that is about $26,000 greater than they could get from one HomeKeeper option, and about $47,000 greater than the other.

But the real difference is greater still, because the HECM creditline is scheduled to grow larger by a projected 7.21% per year while HomeKeeper credit-lines remain flat. So HECM provides even more available cash than either HomeKeeper option.

For example, if these borrowers were to take $10,000 at closing and another $5,000 at the end of the next 10 years (their joint life expectancy from closing is about 19 years), they would retain significantly more available cash from HECM than from either HomeKeeper option.

At roughly halfway to their joint life expectancy (9 years), they would have over $70,000 more credit available from HECM than from either HomeKeeper option. At life expectancy (19 years), they would have over $140,000 still available from HECM, but nothing left from HomeKeeper.

Yet HECM's TALC rates are always less than HomeKeeper's. This is especially pronounced on the day HomeKeeper's equity share goes into effect: the TALC rate of one HomeKeeper option is more than double the HECM TALC, and the other HomeKeeper TALC is more than triple the HECM TALC rate.

(The only private proprietary plan available in Connecticut - Transamerica HomeFirst - would provide about a $54,000 creditline to this couple.)

Table 4: 70-Year-Old Couple in a $300,000 Home in Connecticut (2/98)

	HECM	**HomeKeeper** standard	**HomeKeeper** equity fee
Initial Creditline (at closing)	$82,771	$35,450	$56,475
Annual Growth (initial rate)	7.21%	0%	0%
Creditline Left (assuming $10,000 is taken at closing and another $5,000 per year for the next 10 years) after 3 years	$73,560	$10,450	$31,475
9 years	$75,731	-0-	$1,475
15 years	$107,901	-0-	-0-
19 years	***$142,538***	***-0-***	***-0-***
Total Cost Rate after			
2 years	17.1%	36.4%	26.9%
2 years + 1 day	***17.1%***	***36.4%***	***57.5%***
15 years	8.9%	13.1%	13.7%

Note: Tables 1-4 assume a 4% average annual appreciation rate – the mid-point of the range required by the Truth-in-Lending Act. At 0% appreciation, TALC rates can be much lower, and at 8% appreciation much greater, than the figures in these tables.

Check All Options

Although HECM may be more likely to provide a lot more cash at a lot lower cost on the creditlines most consumers prefer, the best plan for you depends on **your specific situation**. So you need to **consider *all* your reverse mortgage options.** That's especially important if you

- want a monthly loan advance only, or
- live in a home worth more than the median value in your county.

For example, a 75-year-old borrower in a $150,000 home in Kane County, Illinois could get about $100 more per month from HomeKeeper than from HECM. And the annual average cost would be less than HECM during some of the loan term. But in Kankakee County, Illinois - where the median home value is much lower – HomeKeeper's monthly advance would be about $375 greater than HECM's. And the costs would be more competitive as well.

If your home is worth a lot more than the median value in your county, then a private proprietary plan may work the best for you.

The most widely available of these plans (from Transamerica HomeFirst) is being offered in about half the states. It might provide competitive benefits if you want a creditline and your home is worth at least $280,000 ($300,000 for couples) or if you want a monthly advance and your home is worth at least $250,000 ($200,000 for couples).

Chapter 4

Cost Bubbles

Total Annual Loan Cost (TALC) rates are the single best official measure for comparing reverse mortgage costs.

But they do not fully reveal the complete pattern of all loan costs over time. And this can leave you in the dark on some reverse mortgages.

This short but important chapter unveils the significant "cost bubble" that occurs on some HomeKeeper loans, but does not show up on official TALC disclosures.

TALC Rates

Federal Truth-in-Lending law requires disclosure of Total Annual Loan Cost (TALC) rates on all reverse mortgages. As discussed on pages 19-21, these annual average rates generally are greatest in the early years of a loan, and then decline over time. In other words, the true cost is usually greatest in the short term, but then decreases year by year over the life of the loan.

To show how high the cost can be in the short term, federal law requires lenders to show you what the TALC rate would be if the loan were to end two years after closing. They also must show you what it would be if the loan were to end at your life expectancy, and at 40% beyond your life expectancy. (If they want to, they can also show you what the TALC rate would be if the loan ended halfway to your life expectancy.)

Equity-Sharing Fees

To get the greatest loan advances available within the HomeKeeper plan, you must agree to pay an extra "equity-sharing" fee when the loan is over. This fee equals up to 10% of your home's value at that time. If your home were then to be worth $200,000, for example, the fee could be up to an additional $20,000.

The fee goes into effect on the first day of the third year of the loan - one day *after* the short-term TALC disclosure. So this substantial fee is not reflected in the short-term TALC because it isn't charged until one day after the required 2-year disclosure period.

The equity-sharing fee roughly doubles the TALC rate from one day to the next. But the consumer does not see this enormous cost "bubble" because most of it occurs *between* the disclosure periods.

The TALC rate spikes dramatically upward on the day after the short-term (2-year) disclosure. But by the time of the next required TALC projection (life expectancy), most of the bubble has deflated.

Worth a Thousand Words

This chart graphs TALC rates for a 75-year-old in a $200,000 home selecting a creditline HomeKeeper with equity-sharing.

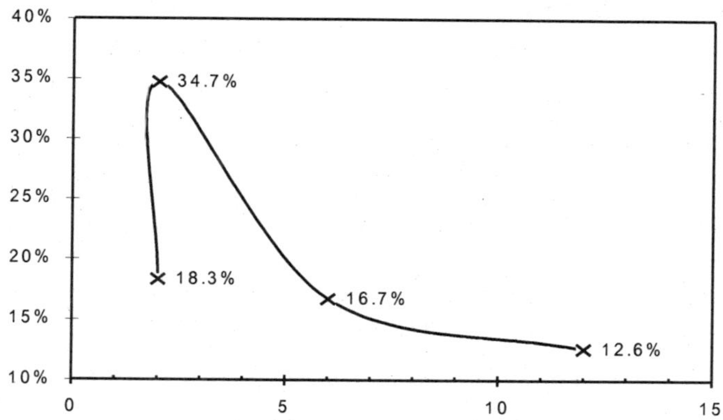

The TALC rate at the required 2-year disclosure period is 18.3%. But it increases to 34.7% on the next day. By the time of the next required disclosure period (12 years), it has declined to 12.6%. But the only rates the consumer sees in the official TALC disclosure are 18.3% and 12.6%.

Current Truth-in-Lending regulations do not require disclosure of the 34.7% - or the significant cost bubble that occurs between 18.3% and 12.6%. Based on official disclosures, you would not know the cost bubble exists.

Indeed, if you knew that in general "TALC rates decline over time," you probably would assume that the 18.3% rate at the end of two years simply decreases straight down to 12.6% at the end of 12 years, with no cost bubble whatsoever.

Poof?

HomeKeeper equity-sharing loans don't always have cost bubbles, and they aren't always full-size.

- If the loan ends within the first two years, you pay no equity-sharing fee. So you get the added benefits without the added cost.
- If your home is worth more than Fannie's equity limit ($227,150 in 1998) at closing, then the fee is less than 10% of your home value at loan maturity.
- Your loan balance plus the equity fee can never exceed the value of your home at loan maturity.

So HomeKeepers with equity-sharing can in some cases have lower TALC rates than comparable Home-Keepers without it. This is more likely to occur if your home value grows at a low rate and you outlive your life expectancy before the loan ends. In Chapters 7 and 8 you will find more resources for comparing HomeKeepers with and without equity-sharing.

Chapter 5

Annuity Choices

A "defined benefit, fixed annuity" sounds complicated. But it's simply a contract with a life insurance company. You pay them a lump sum of cash (the annuity "premium"), and you get a cash payment of a fixed dollar amount (the "defined benefit") every month for the rest of your life.

Using a reverse mortgage to buy *this specific type* of annuity (not any other!) can make sense - if you

- know all your <u>loan</u> options,
- do it for sound reasons,
- understand the cost implications,
- know the public benefit consequences, and
- select a sound plan.

All Your Options

In Chapter 2 you learned that

- you can decide how to have a reverse mortgage loan paid to you, and that
- you can select an immediate cash advance, a creditline, monthly advances, or any combination.

So you know that you don't have to buy an annuity to get fixed monthly cash advances. You can get those from a reverse mortgage without buying an annuity.

Sound Reasons

The main reason for buying an annuity would be to get monthly cash advances for as long as you live - no matter where you live.

Monthly *loan* advances from a reverse mortgage only continue for as long as you live in your present home. You stop getting them if you sell or move. But a defined benefit, fixed annuity pays monthly *annuity* advances without regard to where you live. So the cash advances would continue even if you sold or moved.

If you are concerned about monthly income after moving, or about outliving the cash in a creditline, you might consider an annuity. Or combining monthly annuity advances with a creditline. (Keep in mind, however, that if you move into a nursing home and then qualify for Medicaid, most of the annuity advances would go straight to the nursing home.)

Another reason for considering an annuity is that it might provide more money each month for life than a reverse mortgage would provide each month (in a loan advance) for as long as you live in your home. In some cases, monthly annuity advances can be substantially greater than the monthly loan advances for which a consumer would qualify.

Cost Implications

Loan/annuity combinations are generally more expensive than otherwise comparable loans providing monthly loan advances.

If you use a loan to buy an annuity, you have a larger immediate loan balance. So especially if you die soon, loan/annuity combinations can be a lot more expensive than otherwise comparable loans providing monthly loan advances.

How much more? The only sure way to see the true difference is to compare Total Annual Loan Cost (TALC) rates. *But you must make certain that the annuity is included in the calculation (more on this later).*

Beyond your life expectancy, loan/annuity combinations in some cases can be less expensive than otherwise comparable loans providing monthly loan advances. Especially if you account for the value of ongoing annuity advances past the end of the loan, or any annuity death benefit paid to heirs at that time.

The only reverse mortgage counseling software providing these types of total cost comparisons is NCHEC's "Reverse Mortgage Counselor." Lenders and counselors agreeing to NCHEC's code of conduct (see Chapter 7) get this software at no cost. They can show you how ongoing annuity benefits affect total loan cost rates.

Public Benefit Consequences

Annuity income does not affect your benefits from Social Security or Medicare under current law. But if you are eligible for the Supplemental Security Income (SSI) or Medicaid programs, you need to understand that annuity advances will jeopardize your benefits from these programs.

> ***Annuity advances are counted as income by SSI and Medicaid. So they reduce SSI benefits dollar-for-dollar, and might make you ineligible for Medicaid.***

By contrast, loan advances generally are not counted as income, and not counted as assets if you spend them within the calendar month you receive them.

If you now receive - or expect to become eligible for - SSI or Medicaid, be sure you understand exactly how annuity income would affect your benefits from these programs.

A Sound Plan

You must be very careful to make certain that you consider only

- "defined benefit, fixed" annuities that
- meet Jane Bryant Quinn's safety and soundness criteria,
- provide significant benefits, and are
- offered by companies disclosing TALC rates as defined by federal Truth-in-Lending law.

The only annuity products currently meeting these criteria are the Hartford Lifetime Income Plan and the Transamerica HomeFirst "HouseMoney – Lifetime" plan. (For the latest information, check the "Annuities" page at www.reverse.org.)

- The Hartford plan is only offered in conjunction with "federally-related" reverse mortgages, that is, HECM and HomeKeeper.
- The HomeFirst plan is a "reverse annuity mortgage" that combines an annuity with a private proprietary reverse mortgage.

In some cases, the Hartford plan provides annuity advances for life that are substantially greater than the comparable monthly loan advances you could get for as long as you live in your home from HECM or HomeKeeper. The tables in Chapter 6 present these annuity and loan advances side by side for borrowers of various ages living in homes of various values.

The HomeFirst plan provides its most competitive monthly annuity advances on homes of greater value. If your home is worth more than $250,000 ($200,000 for couples), be sure to get a quote from a HomeFirst lender identified in Chapter 7.

Both plans offer an optional cash refund to your heirs upon your death. This reduces the overall cost of the transaction to your estate. But it also reduces the amount of your fixed monthly annuity advance. Be sure to consider both options carefully.

Other Plans

If you encounter other annuities being offered via reverse mortgage financing, ask to see the annuity's official ratings from the major rating agencies. Then check to see if they meet or exceed at least three of the five ratings listed below, as recommended by Jane Bryant Quinn:

S A. M. Best: A+

S Duff & Phelps: AA+

S Moody's: Aa3

S Standard & Poor's: Aaq

S Weiss: B

If the annuity meets these criteria, please send details on its cost and benefits to NCHEC Annuity, 7373 147 St #115, Apple Valley MN 55124.

Part THREE

Going Shopping

Chapter 6

Got Your Number?

So far you've learned the basics and seen what to look out for. Now it's time to find out what kind of money you could from a reverse mortgage – and what it would cost.

There are three ways to do this:

- for a current, personally customized estimate, use the calculator at **www.reverse.org,**
- for a less precise figure, see the tables in this chapter, or
- for amore precise figure, call one of the counselors or lenders listed in Chapter 7.

Going Online

Calculating your reverse mortgage benefits and costs at **www.reverse.org** is easy. On the "Calculator" page, you just need to type in answers to these questions:

- When were you born?
- When was your spouse (or other co-owner) born?
- How much is your house worth?
- What state do you live in?
- What county do you live in?

> At **www.reverse.org**, go to the "Calculator" page to find out how much cash you could get from a reverse mortgage, and what it would cost.

After you type in this information, you get a quick estimate of the largest amount of cash you could get through the two largest reverse mortgage programs:

- the federally-insured "Home Equity Conversion Mortgage" (HECM), and
- Fannie Mae's "HomeKeeper" mortgage.

These estimates are based on current interest rates, maximum financeable loan fees, and an estimated national average total for third-party closing costs.

Based on these assumptions, the estimates show how much cash you could get from each plan as

- an **Immediate Cash Advance** at loan closing, that is, on the first day of the loan
- OR a **Creditline Account** that lets you withdraw cash at any time after closing
- OR a **Monthly Cash Advance**
    - ❑ for as long as you live in your home
    - ❑ OR (if coupled with an annuity) for life, no matter where you live.

But as you read the estimates online, you need to keep in mind this **important fact**: If you currently owe any debt on your home, and do not pay it off before getting a reverse mortgage, you must take at least that amount as an immediate cash advance at closing, and use it to pay off your debt at that time. If you do not qualify for enough cash to pay off any debt on your home at closing, you cannot get a reverse mortgage.

The online calculator shows you the initial annual rate at which creditlines grow, and project the total amount of available credit that would be left in the future assuming no prior use.

What would it cost?

The online calculator also estimates total cost rates for HECM and HomeKeeper creditline loans based on a projected home appreciation rate of 4% (official disclosures also show the rates at 0% and 8% appreciation as well).

Unlike official disclosures, these estimated total cost rates assume you use all remaining credit on the day the loan ends, so they fully account for the added value of growing creditlines. Also, if you are a couple, these rates are based on joint life expectancy rather than the single life expectancies upon which all official disclosures are based.

Checking the Tables

The tables in this chapter may be the most detailed ones you will find. But they are still tables rather than individually customized, up-to-date estimates like the ones you can get at **www.reverse.org**. So they – like all other tables – are very limited. They may also be misleading because the figures in them are dated, approximate, incomplete, and simplified.

Dated

The tables are based on interest rates in effect during March of 1998. If the rates upon closing a reverse mortgages would be greater, the cash available would be less – all other things being equal. So if rates were to increase sharply, your available cash advances could be much lower than the ones in the tables. But if rates decrease, your available cash would be greater.

> The calculator at **www.reverse.org** is always based on current rates. So you can check it again and again as interest rates change.

Approximate

Reverse mortgage benefits depend on your exact age (or ages) and the exact value of your home. This book would be ALL tables if it showed every combination of ages and home values. Instead, it presents cash advances for selected ages and home values.

So if you aren't exactly 75 and your home isn't worth exactly $150,000, for example, then you have to look at the figures that come closest, and estimate how much greater or lesser your advances might be.

The tables list benefits for single borrowers. But you can also use them to find couples benefits from HECM, which are based on the age of the younger borrower (that is, *as if* the younger borrower were single). HomeKeeper benefits are based on a complex combination of couples' ages (and are much lower for couples). So the tables cannot be used to find HomeKeeper benefits for couples.

> The calculator at **www.reverse.org** uses your precise home value estimate and your exact age(s). So you get an individually customized estimate of your cash benefits.

Incomplete

The tables in this chapter present only the largest cash advances you could get from HECM and HomeKeeper. They don't show you all the choices available in these programs.

Specifically, they present the benefits you could get if you selected a HECM loan in which interest rates can change every month. HECM also lets you choose rates that change only once per year, but the benefits are lower. The tables also only present the HomeKeeper benefits you get if you select Fannie Mae's "equity-sharing" cost option. HomeKeeper benefits without equity-sharing are significantly lower.

More detailed, side-by-side comparative information on all the HECM and HomeKeeper choices is available at no cost, however. (More on that after the tables.) The most widely available proprietary plan is not included in the tables because Transamerica HomeFirst declined to be included in the comparative software that produced them.

Simplified

The amount of cash you can get from the HECM program varies by county, and there are over 3,000 of them in these United States. So the only way you can put together tables that don't go on for thousands of pages is to make some simplifying assumptions.

The main simplifying assumption in this chapter's tables is that your home is not worth more than the median value in your county. So if your home is

- worth more than $86,317 in 1998;
- AND worth more than the median value in your county;
- AND worth less than $170,362 in 1998,

then the HECM figures in the tables may be greater than the amounts for which you could qualify.

A second simplifying assumption is that you do not live in Alaska or Hawaii. If you do, your benefits may be greater than the ones in the tables.

A third assumption is that you will not be misled by the creditline figures. REMEMBER, they are the initial cash amounts available at closing. ***But since it grows larger over time, the HECM creditline can easily provide a lot more cash to you than amount initially available. The HomeKeeper creditline, by contrast, does not grow larger.***

> The calculator at **www.reverse.org** uses your specific county and state to estimate your benefits. So it gives you a more precise estimate no matter where you live. **It also shows you the rate at which the HECM creditline grows, and projects how large it could become in the future.**

But Just Remember This

Now that you've been properly notified about the shortcomings of the tables, you are almost ready to take a look at the next several pages. But only if you promise to remember these three key facts:

- If you currently owe any debt on your home, and do not pay it off before getting a reverse mortgage, you must take at least that amount as an immediate cash advance at closing, and use it to pay off your debt at that time.
  - This would reduce your available creditline by the same dollar amount.
  - Or it would reduce how much you can get as a monthly advance.
  - If you do not qualify for a large enough cash to pay off any debt on your home at closing, you cannot get a reverse mortgage.
- As you look at the tables, please also remember that "what you get" is only one part of the picture. The other important parts are "what you pay" and "what's left" when the loan is over. *You simply cannot make a smart decision until you compare the true total cost of these loans, and the equity you'd have left when it's over.* After the tables, you'll find out where and how you can get this vitally essential information.
- You must also promise to keep in mind that the creditline figures in the tables are the initially available amounts only. So they don't show you the full long-term value of a HECM creditline – which in March of 1998 was growing at an annual rate of 7.4%.

  After the tables, you'll also learn where and how to get the creditline projections you'll need to compare growing HECMs to flat HomeKeepers.

Table 5: Estimated Advances for a **65-Year-Old** Borrower in March of 1998

Home Value	Type of Cash Advance*	HECM	Home Keeper
$75,000	Creditline	$27,757	$16,007
	Monthly (tenure)	183	166
	Monthly (life)	197	108
$100,000	Creditline	$39,582	$22,907
	Monthly (tenure)	260	238
	Monthly (life)	281	155
$150,000	Creditline	$63,232	$36,107
	Monthly (tenure)	416	374
	Monthly (life)	449	244
$200,000	Creditline	$72,863	$49,307
	Monthly (tenure)	480	511
	Monthly (life)	517	333
$250,000	Creditline	$72,863	$56,475
	Monthly (tenure)	480	586
	Monthly (life)	517	381

*HECM creditlines are initially growing larger at 7.4% per year. HomeKeeper creditlines do not grow at all.

"Monthly (tenure)" advances continue for as long as you live in your home.

"Monthly (life)" advances require the purchase of an annuity (see Chapter 5), but annuity advances continue for life - no matter where you live. The figures are based on the Hartford Lifetime Income Plan. The only other loan/annuity plan currently meeting the criteria discussed on pages 44-45 (Transamerica HomeFirst) declined to be included in the comparative software that produced this table.

Table 6: Estimated Advances for a **70-Year-Old** Borrower in March of 1998

Home Value	Type of Cash Advance*	HECM	Home Keeper
$75,000	Creditline	$32,229	$25,342
	Monthly (tenure)	220	230
	Monthly (life)	254	192
$100,000	Creditline	$45,479	$35,492
	Monthly (tenure)	311	322
	Monthly (life)	358	269
$150,000	Creditline	$71,979	$55,192
	Monthly (tenure)	492	501
	Monthly (life)	567	419
$200,000	Creditline	$82,771	$74,892
	Monthly (tenure)	566	679
	Monthly (life)	652	568
$250,000	Creditline	$82,771	$85,589
	Monthly (tenure)	566	776
	Monthly (life)	652	649

*HECM creditlines are initially growing larger at 7.4% per year. HomeKeeper creditlines do not grow at all.

"Monthly (tenure)" advances continue for as long as you live in your home.

"Monthly (life)" advances require the purchase of an annuity (see Chapter 5), but annuity advances continue for life - no matter where you live. The figures are based on the Hartford Lifetime Income Plan. The only other loan/annuity plan currently meeting the criteria discussed on pages 44-45 (Transamerica HomeFirst) declined to be included in the comparative software that produced this table.

Table 7: Estimated Advances for a **75-Year-Old** Borrower in March of 1998

Home Value	Type of Cash Advance*	HECM	Home Keeper
$75,000	Creditline	$37,088	$36,312
	Monthly (tenure)	268	324
	Monthly (life)	331	317
$100,000	Creditline	$51,863	$50,137
	Monthly (tenure)	375	447
	Monthly (life)	463	438
$150,000	Creditline	$81,413	$77,187
	Monthly (tenure)	589	689
	Monthly (life)	727	674
$200,000	Creditline	$93,447	$104,237
	Monthly (tenure)	676	930
	Monthly (life)	835	911
$250,000	Creditline	$93,447	$118,925
	Monthly (tenure)	676	1,061
	Monthly (life)	835	1,039

*HECM creditlines are initially growing larger at 7.4% per year. HomeKeeper creditlines do not grow at all.

"Monthly (tenure)" advances continue for as long as you live in your home.

"Monthly (life)" advances require the purchase of an annuity (see Chapter 5), but annuity advances continue for life - no matter where you live. The figures are based on the Hartford Lifetime Income Plan. The only other loan/annuity plan currently meeting the criteria discussed on pages 44-45 (Transamerica HomeFirst) declined to be included in the comparative software that produced this table.

Table 8: Estimated Advances for an **80-Year-Old** Borrower in March of 1998

Home Value	Type of Cash Advance*	HECM	Home Keeper
$75,000	Creditline	$42,222	$43,136
	Monthly (tenure)	334	422
	Monthly (life)	452	455
$100,000	Creditline	$58,572	$59,136
	Monthly (tenure)	463	579
	Monthly (life)	627	624
$150,000	Creditline	$91,272	$90,536
	Monthly (tenure)	721	886
	Monthly (life)	977	956
$200,000	Creditline	$104,589	$121,936
	Monthly (tenure)	827	1,194
	Monthly (life)	1,119	1,287
$250,000	Creditline	$104,589	$138,986
	Monthly (tenure)	827	1,361
	Monthly (life)	1,119	1,467

*HECM creditlines are initially growing larger at 7.4% per year. HomeKeeper creditlines do not grow at all.

"Monthly (tenure)" advances continue for as long as you live in your home.

"Monthly (life)" advances require the purchase of an annuity (see Chapter 5), but annuity advances continue for life - no matter where you live. The figures are based on the Hartford Lifetime Income Plan. The only other loan/annuity plan currently meeting the criteria discussed on pages 44-45 (Transamerica HomeFirst) declined to be included in the comparative software that produced this table.

Table 9: Estimated Advances for an **85-Year-Old** Borrower in March of 1998

Home Value	Type of Cash Advance*	HECM	Home Keeper
$75,000	Creditline	$47,536	$49,614
	Monthly (tenure)	433	576
	Monthly (life)	629	656
$100,000	Creditline	$65,461	$67,614
	Monthly (tenure)	597	784
	Monthly (life)	866	894
$150,000	Creditline	$101,311	$103,014
	Monthly (tenure)	924	1,195
	Monthly (life)	1,340	1,362
$200,000	Creditline	$115,911	$138,414
	Monthly (tenure)	1,057	1,606
	Monthly (life)	1,533	1,830
$250,000	Creditline	$115,911	$157,636
	Monthly (tenure)	1,057	1,829
	Monthly (life)	1,533	2,084

*HECM creditlines are initially growing larger at 7.4% per year. HomeKeeper creditlines do not grow at all.

"Monthly (tenure)" advances continue for as long as you live in your home.

"Monthly (life)" advances require the purchase of an annuity (see Chapter 5), but annuity advances continue for life - no matter where you live. The figures are based on the Hartford Lifetime Income Plan. The only other loan/annuity plan currently meeting the criteria discussed on pages 44-45 (Transamerica HomeFirst) declined to be included in the comparative software that produced this table.

Table 10: Estimated Advances for a **90-Year-Old** Borrower in March of 1998

Home Value	Type of Cash Advance*	HECM	Home Keeper
$75,000	Creditline	$52,736	$50,169
	Monthly (tenure)	618	741
	Monthly (life)	892	849
$100,000	Creditline	$72,111	$68,169
	Monthly (tenure)	844	1,007
	Monthly (life)	1,220	1,153
$150,000	Creditline	$110,861	$103,569
	Monthly (tenure)	1,298	1,530
	Monthly (life)	1,876	1,752
$200,000	Creditline	$126,642	$138,969
	Monthly (tenure)	1,483	2,053
	Monthly (life)	2,143	2,351
$250,000	Creditline	$126,642	$158,191
	Monthly (tenure)	1,483	2,336
	Monthly (life)	2,143	2,677

*HECM creditlines are initially growing larger at 7.4% per year. HomeKeeper creditlines do not grow at all.

"Monthly (tenure)" advances continue for as long as you live in your home.

"Monthly (life)" advances require the purchase of an annuity (see Chapter 5), but annuity advances continue for life - no matter where you live. The figures are based on the Hartford Lifetime Income Plan. The only other loan/annuity plan currently meeting the criteria discussed on pages 44-45 (Transamerica HomeFirst) declined to be included in the comparative software that produced this table.

Calling Counselors & Lenders

The tables and **www.reverse.org** give you two ways to estimate how much cash you could get from a reverse mortgage. A third way is to call one of the counselors or lenders listed in Chapter 7.

These local sources can give you the ***most accurate estimates*** *of all because they know the exact loan fees and third-party closing costs that would be charged on your loan.* (The figures in the tables and online assume maximum financeable fees and an approximate national average of third-party closing costs.)

Some of the lenders listed in the next chapter can also show you the costs and benefits of private, proprietary products. If your home is worth a lot more than the median value in your county, one of these products might provide a lot more cash than either HECM or HomeKeeper.

All of the counseling agencies and lenders in Chapter 7 can prepare for you a free "Personal Reverse Mortgage Analysis." This 12-page report lays out all your HECM and HomeKeeper options, including combinations of immediate cash advances, creditlines, and monthly advances. It compares total cost rates and leftover equity as well. Learn where to get yours in the very next chapter.

Chapter 7

Where to Look

"If you or anyone in your life might need a reverse mortgage, there's only one smart place to look: a lender with the seal of approval of the nonprofit National Center for Home Equity Conversion (NCHEC)."

Jane Bryant Quinn
The Washington Post

"Order the latest list of 'preferred' counselors and lenders from the nonprofit National Center for Home Equity Conversion."

AARP Home Equity
Information Center

Preferred Providers

To promote important standards for the reverse mortgage market, and to help consumers find agencies and companies pledging to uphold those standards, the National Center for Home Equity Conversion (NCHEC) (see page 131) recognizes "preferred" counselors and lenders.

NCHEC-Preferred Counselors are employees of non-profit or public agencies and pledge to abide by NCHEC's Counselor Code of Conduct. NCHEC-Preferred Lenders offer federally-insured reverse mortgages and pledge to abide by NCHEC's Lender Code of Conduct.

Preferred Counselors Pledge

- **TO DISCLOSE ALL YOUR OPTIONS**
  At your request, we will prepare for you an individually customized Personal Reverse Mortgage Analysis - an objective report covering a range of reverse mortgage choices and other alternatives. (This report is produced by a computer software program provided to us at no cost by NCHEC.)

- **TO BE UNBIASED**
  We will provide a schedule of any fees we charge or any related payments or donations made to us by others. None of our counseling income depends on whether or not you take a reverse mortgage. We do not accept payments or donations in exchange for altering our counseling standards.

- **TO BE INDEPENDENT**
  We will not steer you to a specific lender, loan, or other option. We will respect your decisions on the choices we present. Only you can decide what's right for you and best meets your needs.

- **TO PROTECT YOUR PRIVACY**
  We will not give personal information about you to outside parties without your permission.

Preferred Lenders Pledge

- **TO DISCLOSE ALL YOUR OPTIONS**
  At your request and at no charge, we will prepare for you an individually customized Personal Reverse Mortgage Analysis - an objective report covering a range of reverse mortgage choices and other alternatives. (This report is produced by a computer software program provided to us at no cost by NCHEC.)

- **TO RESPECT YOUR DECISIONS**
  We will not pressure you into making any decision. Only you can decide what's right for you and best meets your needs. We will honor your decisions on all of the choices in the programs we offer.

- **TO PROTECT YOUR PRIVACY**
  We will not give personal information about you to outside parties without your permission.

Counselors and lenders pay nothing for their "NCHEC-Preferred" status. So they cannot "buy" their way onto NCHEC's preferred provider list.

They are licensed to use NCHEC's "Reverse Mortgage Counselor" computer software at no cost to them. This software generates a 12-page "Personal Reverse Mortgage Analysis" - the most detailed comparative information on reverse mortgages and other options now available.

Getting great information service that helps you make the best decisions is your most important need in this market. As you learned in Part TWO, seeing all the information presented fairly could make a major difference in what you decide.

That's why it's smart to deal with lenders and counselors who can generate and explain clearly the specific information you need.

In Chapter 8 you will learn all about the "Personal Reverse Mortgage Analysis" and the additional types of detailed, individually-customized information that NCHEC's "Reverse Mortgage Counselor" software provides.

The rest of this chapter presents the counselors and lenders agreeing to NCHEC's codes of conduct and offering the 12-page "Personal Reverse Mortgage Analysis" as of March, 1998.

For the very latest version of the NCHEC preferred provider codes and lists, see "Standards" and "Sources" at **www.reverse.org**.

Preferred Counselors

ARIZONA
ARC 602-241-6169; 520-327-8250

CALIFORNIA
Consumer Credit Counseling 805-383-7700
ECHO Housing 510-271-7931; 510-679-8023
Human Investment 415-348-6660
Inland Mediation 909-984-2254
Neighborhood House 619-263-7761

COLORADO
Family Counseling 719-544-4233

DELAWARE
Neighborhood House 302-652-3928

FLORIDA
Catholic Charities 904-354-4846
CCCS Gulf Coast 800-741-7040
Back to Top

GEORGIA
Dekalb-Fulton Housing Counseling 404-508-0922

ILLINOIS
CEDA of Cook Co 312-795-8961
NHS of Kankakee 815-939-9700

INDIANA
HAND 812-349-3401
HUD 317-226-7036

MICHIGAN
Oakland Co Housing 810-858-5402

MINNESOTA
Senior Housing 612-331-4063

MISSOURI
HOPE 314-776-0155

NORTH CAROLINA
Mid-East Commission 919-946-8043

NORTH DAKOTA
CAA 701-232-2452; 800-726-7960

NEW JERSEY
Atlantic Co Intergenerational 888-426-9243
Bergen Co Senior Services 201-646-2625

NEW YORK
Cornell Extension 518-885-8995
Family Service 516-485-5600
Essex Co Housing 518-873-6888
Metro Interfaith 607-772-6766
Tompkins Co Aging 607-274-5492

OHIO
Better Housing 513-721-6855
Catholic Charities 440-998-6264
Housing Directions 419-535-7272

PENNSYLVANIA
CAP Counseling 610-375-7866
Indiana County CAP 412-465-2657
NW Counseling 215-324-7500
Trehab Center 800-982-4045

SOUTH CAROLINA
Urban League 864-244-3862
Palmetto Legal 803-799-9668

VIRGINIA
Crater AAA 804-732-7020
STOP, Inc. 757-858-1360
Valley Aging Services 540-949-7141

WASHINGTON
Aberdeen NHS 360-533-7828
Fremont Public Association 206-273-9181
SNAP 509-456-7106

Preferred Lenders

All NCHEC-Preferred Lenders offer federally-insured (HECM) reverse mortgages. Other offerings are indicate by these abbreviations:

F = Fannie Mae HomeKeeper

H = Hartford Lifetime Income Plan

N = Financial Freedom

T = Transamerica HomeFirst

Financial Freedom **(N)** and Transamerica Home-First **(T)** are private proprietary plans that generally are more costly and provide their most competitive benefits on more expensive homes. For a general estimate of when to consider these plans, see the bottom of page 34. For more on the HomeFirst **(T)** and Hartford **(H)** plans, see Chapter 5.

ALABAMA
Amerifirst Mortgage 800-473-6467
Homestead Mortgage FT 800-941-2274
Norwest Mortgage F 800-336-7359
Unity Mortgage F 800-588-8044

ALASKA
GMAC Mortgage FH 888-737-4622
Norwest Mortgage FH 800-336-7359
Seattle Mortgage FT 800-640-1626 x224; 800-643-6610 x9; 907-562-5626 x224

ARIZONA
Farwest Mortgage FT 602-661-5545; 602-816-4564
Financial Freedom FHN 800-500-5150
First Mortgage F 888-608-5868
GMAC Mortgage FH 888-737-4622
Norwest Mortgage FH 800-336-7359
Sun American F 800-469-7383
Unity Mortgage F 800-334-9057
WestAmerica Mortgage F 800-999-2649

ARKANSAS
Amerifirst Mortgage 800-473-6467
GMAC Mortgage H 888-737-4622
Norwest Mortgage FH 800-336-7359
Unity Mortgage F 800-336-3135

CALIFORNIA

Farwest Mortgage FT 510-462-3732; 619-967-6951; 714-579-1177; 805-928-6711; 909-621-1908
Financial Freedom FHN 800-500-5150
GMAC Mortgage FHT 888-737-4622
Metrociti Mortgage FHT 800-464-2484
National Pacific F 209-474-6161;310-527-2055; 562-402-8400; 707-546-4356; 714-978-6762; 800-545-4848; 800-899-3070; 805-253-1133; 805-543-2727; 805-981-8600; 818-787-7720
Neighbors Financial F 916-732-2340
Norwest Mortgage FHT 800-336-7359
Senior Loan Center FHT 800-423-4222
Unity Mortgage FT 800-334-9057
Village Home Loans FT 408-274-3333
West Coast Mortgage FHT 800-625-5626

COLORADO

Financial Freedom FHN 800-500-5150
GMAC Mortgage FHT 888-737-4622
Norwest Mortgage FH 800-318-0826
Unity Mortgage FT 800-358-8012
WestAmerica Mortgage F 800-999-2649

CONNECTICUT

ACE Mortgages FT 800-881-2954
Amerifirst Mortgage FT 800-473-6467
Amston Mortgage FT 800-625-8633
BNY Mortgage FT 800-269-6797
GMAC Mortgage FHT 888-737-4622
Hartford Funding FT 888-241-5100
Norwest Mortgage FHT 800-336-7359
Unity Mortgage FT 800-203-4667

DELAWARE
Amerifirst Mortgage FT 800-473-6467
Boulevard Mortgage FT 800-767-5664; 215-633-8080
GMAC Mortgage FH 888-737-4622
International Mortgage FHT 800-581-7806
Lincoln Mortgage F 800-480-0050 x233
Norwest Mortgage FH 800-336-7359
Phoenix Mortgage F 800-427-0800
Unity Mortgage F 800-368-3254

DISTRICT OF COLUMBIA
Amerifirst Mortgage FT 800-473-6467
GMAC Mortgage FHT 888-737-4622
International Mortgage FHT 800-581-7806
Norwest Mortgage FHT 8-336-7359
Unity Mortgage FT 800-368-3254

FLORIDA
America's Senior Financial Svcs. FHT 800-760-5363
Amerifirst Mortgage 800-473-6467
GMAC Mortgage FHT 888-737-4622
Homestead Mortgage FT 800-941-2274
Lincoln Mortgage FT 888-435-7353
Norwest Mortgage FHT 800-445-0520
Pinnacle Financial FT 800-421-5626
Unity Mortgage FT 800-588-8044

GEORGIA
Amerifirst Mortgage 800-473-6467
GMAC Mortgage FHT 888-737-4622
Homestead Mortgage FT 800-941-2274
Mortgage South 800-866-1707
Norwest Mortgage FHT 800-336-7359
Unity Mortgage FT 800-588-8044

HAWAII
GMAC Mortgage HT 888-737-4622
Norwest Mortgage FH 800-336-7359

IDAHO
Amerifirst Mortgage 800-473-6467
GMAC Mortgage H 888-737-4622
Norwest Mortgage FH 800-336-7359
Seattle Mortgage FT 800-643-6610 x9
Unity Mortgage FT 800-334-9057

ILLINOIS
Amerifirst Mortgage 800-473-6467
Berkshire Mortgage F 800-323-3404
Custom Mortgage F 800-729-7937
GMAC Mortgage FHT 888-737-4622
Norwest Mortgage FHT 800-603-9959
Unity Mortgage FT 800-880-7740
WestAmerica Mortgage F 800-999-2649

INDIANA
American Mortgage FT 888-395-7165
Berkshire Mortgage F 800-323-3404
Custom Mortgage F 800-729-7937
GMAC Mortgage FH 888-737-4622
Homeowners Mortgage F 800-926-5406
Norwest Mortgage FH 800-336-7359
Transamerica HomeFirst F 800-538-5569
Unity Mortgage FT 800-860-6983
WestAmerica Mortgage F 800-999-2649

IOWA
Allied Group Mortgage F 800-356-3442
Amerifirst Mortgage 800-473-6467
GMAC Mortgage FH 888-737-4622

IOWA, continued
Norwest Mortgage FH 800-603-9959
WestAmerica Mortgage F 800-999-2649
Unity Mortgage F 800-880-7740
WestAmerica Mortgage F 800-999-2649

KANSAS
GMAC Mortgage H 888-737-4622
James B Nutter F 800-798-3946
Norwest Mortgage FH 800-538-1620
Transamerica HomeFirst F 800-538-5569
Unity Mortgage F 800-336-3135

KENTUCKY
American Mortgage FT 888-395-7165
Amerifirst Mortgage 800-473-6467
Custom Mortgage F 800-729-7937
GMAC Mortgage FH 888-737-4622
Norwest Mortgage FH 800-336-7359
Tri-County Mortgage F 800-455-5581
Unity Mortgage FT 800-860-6983

LOUISIANA
Amerifirst Mortgage 800-473-6467
GMAC Mortgage H 888-737-4622
Norwest Mortgage FH 800-336-7359
Unity Mortgage F 800-336-3135

MAINE
GMAC Mortgage H 888-737-4622
Norwest Mortgage FH 800-336-7359
Unity Mortgage F 800-203-4667

MARYLAND
Amerifirst Mortgage FT 800-473-6467
GMAC Mortgage FHT 888-737-4622

MARYLAND, continued
International Mortgage FHT 800-581-7806
Norwest Mortgage FHT 800-336-7359
Unity Mortgage FT 800-368-3254

MASSACHUSETTS
Amerifirst Mortgage 800-473-6467
Amston Mortgage 800-625-8633
GMAC Mortgage H 888-737-4622
Hartford Funding 888-241-5100
Norwest Mortgage H 800-336-7359
Unity Mortgage 800-203-4667

MICHIGAN
Custom Mortgage F 800-729-7937
GMAC Mortgage FHT 888-737-4622
Norwest Mortgage FHT 800-336-7359
Unity Mortgage FT 800-860-6983

MINNESOTA
GMAC Mortgage FH 888-737-4622
Heigl Mortgage F 888-831-6644
Norwest Mortgage FH 800-995-0426
Richfield Bank F 612-798-3339
Unity Mortgage FT 800-880-7740

MISSISSIPPI
Amerifirst Mortgage 800-473-6467
GMAC Mortgage H 888-737-4622
Norwest Mortgage FH 601-453-5044
Unity Mortgage F 800-588-8044

MISSOURI
Amerifirst Mortgage 800-473-6467
Custom Mortgage F 800-729-7937
GMAC Mortgage FH 888-737-4622

MISSOURI, continued
James B Nutter F 800-798-3946
Norwest Mortgage FH 800-538-1620
Transamerica HomeFirst F 800-538-5569
Unity Mortgage 800-336-3135

MONTANA
GMAC Mortgage H 888-737-4622
Norwest Mortgage FH 800-336-7359
Unity Mortgage F 800-334-9057

NEBRASKA
Amerifirst Mortgage 800-473-6467
GMAC Mortgage H 888-737-4622
Norwest Mortgage FH 800-336-7359
Unity Mortgage F 800-358-8012

NEVADA
GMAC Mortgage FH 888-737-4622
Norwest Mortgage FH 702-454-2870; 702-686-2062
Unity Mortgage F 800-334-9057

NEW HAMPSHIRE
GMAC Mortgage FH 888-737-4622
Norwest Mortgage FH 800-336-7359
Providian National Bank F 800-537-4332
Unity Mortgage F 800-203-4667

NEW JERSEY
Amerifirst Mortgage FT 800-473-6467
BNY Mortgage FT 800-269-6797
GMAC Mortgage FHT 888-737-4622
Lincoln Mortgage FT 800-480-0050 x233
Norwest Mortgage FH 800-336-7359
Phoenix Mortgage FT 800-427-0800
Unity Mortgage F 800-487-0088

NEW MEXICO
Amerifirst Mortgage 800-473-6467
GMAC Mortgage H 888-737-4622
Norwest Mortgage FH 505-237-2859
Unity Mortgage F 800-358-8012

NEW YORK
ACE Mortgages FT 800-881-2954
Amerifirst Mortgage FT 800-473-6467
Amston Mortgage F 800-625-8633
BNY Mortgage FT 800-269-6797
GMAC Mortgage FHT 888-737-4622
Hartford Funding FT 888-241-5100
Norwest Mortgage FHT 800-336-7359
Unity Mortgage F 800-203-4667

NORTH CAROLINA
Amerifirst Mortgage 800-473-6467
Centura Bank 800-879-5864
GMAC Mortgage H 888-737-4622
Norwest Mortgage H 800-336-7359
Unity Mortgage 800-588-8044

NORTH DAKOTA
GMAC Mortgage H 888-737-4622
Norwest Mortgage FH 800-336-7359

OHIO
American Mortgage FT 888-395-7165
Amerifirst Mortgage 800-473-6467
Custom Mortgage F 800-729-7937
Excel Mortgage FT 216-573-8090
GMAC Mortgage FHT 888-737-4622
Hartford Funding F 888-241-5100
Norwest Mortgage FHT 800-336-7359
Unity Mortgage FT 800-860-6983

OKLAHOMA
Amerifirst Mortgage F 800-473-6467
GMAC Mortgage H 888-737-4622
Norwest Mortgage FH 800-336-7359
Unity Mortgage F 800-336-3135

OREGON
GMAC Mortgage FT 888-737-4622
National Pacific F 800-640-4773
Norwest Mortgage F 503-585-8082
Seattle Mortgage FT 800-643-6610 x9
Unity Mortgage FT 800-334-9057

PENNSYLVANIA
Boulevard Mortgage FT 800-767-5664; 215-633-8080
GMAC Mortgage FHT 888-737-4622
International Mortgage FHT 800-581-7806
Lincoln Mortgage FT 800-480-0050 x233
Norwest Mortgage FHT 800-805-9142
Phoenix Mortgage FT 800-427-0800
Unity Mortgage F 800-487-0088

RHODE ISLAND
GMAC Mortgage FH 888-737-4622
Norwest Mortgage FH 800-336-7359
Rhode Island Housing 401-751-5566
Unity Mortgage F 800-203-4667

SOUTH CAROLINA
Amerifirst Mortgage 800-473-6467
GMAC Mortgage H 888-737-4622
Norwest Mortgage FH 800-336-7359
Unity Mortgage F 800-588-8044

SOUTH DAKOTA
Norwest Mortgage FH 800-336-7359

TENNESSEE
Amerifirst Mortgage 800-473-6467
GMAC Mortgage H 888-737-4622
Mortgage South 800-866-1707
Norwest Mortgage FH 800-336-7359
Unity Mortgage 800-588-8044

TEXAS (see page 9)

UTAH
Amerifirst Mortgage 800-473-6467
C & B Financial FHT 801-685-8913
GMAC Mortgage H 888-737-4622
Norwest Mortgage FH 800-336-7359
Sun American F 801-256-0802; 888-256-0878
Unity Mortgage F 800-358-8012

VERMONT
GMAC Mortgage H 888-737-4622
Norwest Mortgage FH 800-336-7359
Unity Mortgage F 800-203-4667

VIRGINIA
GMAC Mortgage FHT 888-737-4622
International Mortgage FHT 800-581-7806
Norwest Mortgage FHT 800-336-7359
Unity Mortgage FT 800-368-3254

WASHINGTON
Cascade Bank F 800-326-8787
Financial Freedom FHN 800-500-5150
GMAC Mortgage FHT 888-737-4622

WASHINGTON, continued
Norwest Mortgage FHT 800-329-6400;
206-778-3402; 509-276-8536
Seattle Mortgage FT 800-643-6610 x9;
206-281-1500 x9; 509-448-0771
Unity Mortgage FT 800-334-9057

WEST VIRGINIA
GMAC Mortgage H 888-737-4622
International Mortgage FHT 800-581-7806
Norwest Mortgage FH 800-336-7359
Unity Mortgage F 800-368-3254

WISCONSIN
GMAC Mortgage FH 888-737-4622
Norwest Mortgage FH 414-231-4625
Transamerica HomeFirst F 800-538-5569
Unity Mortgage F 800-880-7740

WYOMING
GMAC Mortgage H 888-737-4622
Norwest Mortgage FH 800-336-7359
Unity Mortgage F 800-358-8012

Chapter 8

What to Ask

Start by asking any NCHEC-preferred counselor or lender to prepare for you a free, individually-customized "Personal Reverse Mortgage Analysis."

This 12-page report will be based on your specific situation: your age (or ages), your life expectancy, your home's value and location, current interest rates, your choices and preferences. It will show you

- detailed side-by-side comparisons of all your major reverse mortgage choices
- specific cash advance amounts, total loan costs, and leftover equity for you or your heirs

- all the consumer information required by federal reverse mortgage counseling law
- special details on loan costs not covered by federal truth-in-Lending disclosures
- information on non-debt and other options available in your state
- details on home appreciation rates in your state over the past year, past five years, and since 1980
- the consumer economics of selling your specific home and moving at your current age and life expectancy.

Asking Providers

Read the analysis carefully. Check the **origination fees** on the "Summary of Loan Terms" (page 12) to see how much money the lender will earn for setting up each loan. Ask questions about anything on any page. But don't stop there.

The "Reverse Mortgage Counselor" software that produces the report can answer a whole range of additional questions as well. So ask preferred providers any "what-if" questions you'd like answered. Here's some examples:

- If your are interested in a growing HECM creditline:

  "If I took out this much cash now and that much cash then *(tell them how much and when),* how much cash would remain available to me at various future times, and how would that compare with the remaining cash left in a flat HomeKeeper creditline?"

- If you want to see how total loan costs compare:

  "Can you show me a chart that graphs the TALC rates on these loans, including the 'cost bubble' from HomeKeeper's equity fee?"

- If you want to see how your debt and equity would change over time:

  "Can you show me a chart that graphs my future debt and leftover equity on a specific loan?"

  "What would I owe and how much equity would I have left if I sold and moved at various future times?

  "How would those figures change if you assume the value of my home grows at the average annual appreciation rate for my state over the past year, past five years, or since 1980?" *(Or any other rate you choose.)*

- If you are a single male or a couple:

  "TALC rates assume all borrowers are single females. What would the rates be if they were based on the life expectancy of a single male my age (or of a couple our ages)?"

- If you are interested in monthly advances:

  "TALC rates do not take into account the value of an annuity beyond the end of a loan. What would the rates be if they did?"

  "At what combination of home appreciation and loan term would an equity-sharing HomeKeeper have lower TALCs than a comparable HomeKeeper without equity-sharing?"

Answers to these types of questions may be very helpful to you. And they might be vitally important to you and your pocketbook. So don't be shy. Preferred providers have the software that can easily answer these types of questions. Ask away!

Asking Yourself

The most important questions we ask are often the ones we ask ourselves. How do we feel about debt, spending, and investing? How do we determine the value of something?

What about "borrowing"?

Many of us have been well served by these borrowing cautions:

- ❑ don't borrow in general
- ❑ don't borrow against your home in particular

"**Don't Borrow**" Borrowing usually means using money you haven't earned yet. You borrow today in the hope that you will be able to earn enough in the future to repay it. So you are borrowing against your uncertain future earnings - which sounds like "counting your chickens before they hatch." That's generally not a good idea unless you have a steady job.

But this caution doesn't really apply to reverse mortgages because you are not borrowing against future income. In fact, you are borrowing against home equity that you have already earned. So you aren't counting your chickens before they hatch. You are hatching the nest egg you've already earned.

"**Not Against Your Home**" Borrowing against your home usually means paying back a loan every month. But if you lose your job or your income drops, you could miss some payments and lose your home to foreclosure. That's why it's generally not a good idea to borrow against your home unless it's for a very basic purpose. You want avoid jeopardizing your home ownership.

But this caution doesn't apply to reverse mortgages either, because no monthly repayment is required. You can't lose your home by missing a payment because there are none to make.

What about "spending"?

Many of us have also been well served by these spending cautions: "You don't know how much you will need and how long you will live. So don't spend your savings. Wait till you really need them."

Makes a lot of sense. But - if you literally followed these cautions forever, you would never use any of the money you spend a lifetime building up. And that doesn't make much sense. Why go to the trouble of earning it and saving it if you're never going to use any of it?

So in retirement, this spending caution should be converted into these questions:

- when should you consider using how much savings?
- which savings (for example, home equity)?

As amended, this caution clearly does apply to reverse mortgages. Because the more home equity "savings" you use now, the less you'll have later. So the questions now become:

If you ever do take a reverse mortgage, should you do it now or wait until later to decide? (In the future, you may be eligible for more cash because you will be older and your home may be worth more. On the other hand, interest rates may be higher, and that would decrease the amount otherwise available.)

If you take one now, how should you take it: creditline, monthly, or a combination? If you take a creditline, how much of it should you use now versus later? If you take a monthly advance, should you select a specific number of years, for as long as you live in your home, or should you buy an annuity providing lifetime advances no matter where you live?

What about "investing"?

Should you use a reverse mortgage to invest in financial products providing variable, uncertain returns? Generally a lousy idea - unless, of course, you can afford to lose money.

- Remember, to come out ahead on any variable investment, you'd have to earn a greater rate of return on it than the TALC rate you are paying on the loan. And the odds against doing that safely are mighty long.
- A much better alternative is to take a HECM creditline. You only get charged interest on the cash advances you've actually taken, and the remaining available credit grows larger every month. And this growth is not an "interest" earning, so you are not taxed on it.

What's it worth?

Only you can decide what a reverse mortgage might be worth to you. It probably depends most on what you would use one for: increasing your monthly income, having a cash reserve (creditline account) for irregular or unexpected expenses, paying off debt that requires monthly repayments, repairing or improving your home, getting the services you need to remain independent, improving the quality of your life.

One approach is to consider a major alternative: selling your home and moving. Do you have any idea

- how much money you could get by selling your home?

- what it would cost to buy and maintain or rent a new one?
- how much you could safely earn on sale proceeds not used for a new home?

Your "Personal Reverse Mortgage Analysis" estimates how much cash you could spend on housing each month using proceeds from the sale of your home. Use this estimate to look into other housing options. Seeing them first-hand and in-person may help you decide about a reverse mortgage.

- You may find a different home, neighborhood, or community with an array of services or amenities that is much more attractive than you would expect to find.
- Or, you may only confirm what you were pretty sure of all along: that where you live now is easily the best place for you to be.

Either way, looking will give you a much better idea of the overall costs and benefits of staying versus moving. That will give you a better sense of what's valuable to you. And make it easier to evaluate the cost of a reverse mortgage.

Also take a look at other financial and services options that you may prefer instead of - or decide to combine with - a reverse mortgage. You'll find a guide to these alternatives in Chapter 9.

Chapter 9

Other Options

Taking a reverse mortgage is a big step. So now is the time to consider all your other options as well. You just might find a better solution. Or you might find a solution that makes sense in addition to a reverse mortgage. This chapter introduces you to a variety of other choices.

To get all the information on these options, use the "Related Options" page at **www.reverse.org**. It links you directly into the very best and most helpful related websites.

Financial Options

- Roughly one-half of all Americans aged 65+ who are eligible for monthly cash benefits from Supplemental Security Income (SSI) are not getting them!

> Link directly into the SSI website from the "Related Options" page at **www.reverse.org** to see if you qualify. This page also links you to SSI state supplements if you live in CA, DC, HI, MA, NV, NJ, NY, PA, RI, VT, or WA.

- Find out if you qualify for a low-cost property tax deferral loan by calling the local office to which you send your property tax payments if you live in CA, CO, CT, DC, FL, GA, IL, IA, ME, MD, MA, MI, MN, ND, NH, OR, SD, TN, TX, UT, VA, WA, WI, OR WY. Eligibility criteria vary, benefits in some cases are limited to special assessments, and not all programs are available on a statewide basis.
- Credit problems? Need sound investment advice?

> Link directly to the National Foundation for Consumer Credit and the American Association of Individual Investors from the "Related Options" page.

Housing Options

- Need affordable financing for a home repair, improvement, or modification?

> Link directly from "Related Options" at www.reverse.org to the National Directory of Home Modification & Repair Programs. Its national map can take you straight to details on programs in your community.

- Wondering how much your home is worth? You could ask realtors for estimates. Or you could get an on-line appraisal:

> Link directly from the "Related Options" page to Experian to get an online estimate of your home's value for as little as $8.

- Curious about other housing options in your area – or anyplace else?

> Link directly from "Related Options" to the American Association of Homes and Services for the Aging (AAHSA) and SeniorSites.

Services Options

- The single best source of information on a wide range of local programs and services is your local Area Agency on Aging (AAA). To find the AAA nearest you call1-800-677-1116. Or go online to search the single best national database of local programs and services:

> Link directly from the "Related Options" page at www.reverse.org to the Eldercare Locator - the most comprehensive source for local programs and services.

- Need legal help?

> Link directly to a wealth of legal resources at the National Senior Citizens Law Center or find an attorney through the National Association of Elderlaw Attorneys.

- And don't forget AARP:

> Link directly to the very best general source of informational resources at www.aarp.org.

Part FOUR

Learning More

Chapter 10

More Resources

Need still more information? This chapter presents organizations and materials that may be helpful to you in getting what you need.

- The organizational contacts have special expertise or responsibilities in the reverse mortgage market.
- The materials have been carefully selected from a vast array of candidates, and are categorized to help you find what you need.

Organizations

Consumer Counselors

If there are no NCHEC-Preferred Counselors in your area, call 1-800-569-4287 for HUD counselors offering HECM counseling. These agencies vary widely in counseling competence, and generally do not yet have the computer resources to provide the detailed information you may need to make a fully informed decision.

> Link directly from the "Contacts" page at **www.reverse.org** into the Housing Counseling Clearinghouse website to find HECM counselors.

Consumer Organizations

- American Association of Retired Persons (AARP)
  Home Equity Info Center: 202-434-6044
  Federal Policy: 202-434-3770
- American Bar Association (ABA)
  Commission on Legal Problems of the Elderly: 202-662-8690
- National Center for Home Equity Conversion (NCHEC): 612-953-4474; 612-953-3230 (fax)

Government Agencies

- U. S. Dept. of Housing and Urban Development
  HECM Program: 202-708-2700
  Legal: 202-708-0080
  Policy Development & Research: 202-708-0421

Industry Contacts

> For a current directory of industry contacts, including companies providing reverse mortgage loan products, training, table funding, contract servicing, legal and regulatory research, servicing software, and market research, see the "Contacts" page at **www.reverse.org.**

Private Consultants

- Ibis Capital: origination and disclosure software, portfolio and servicing analysis, product design; 415-563-3367

- NCHEC: consumer education and information, public policy analysis, consumer economic analysis, public incentives for home equity financing of long term care, counselor training, consumer publications and software, public relations consultation, internet consultation and website development; 612-953-4474

Materials

Consumer Info

AARP Foundation. **Reverse Mortgage Choices**.

- Two 15-minute videotapes: a general introduction, and a closer look. Written by Ken Scholen; featuring Scholen and Bronwyn Belling.
- The two tapes are combined on a single VHS cartridge and come with a Video Resource Guide.
- Send $5.00 for the complete package to AARP Foundation, P O Box 51040 GASD, Washington, DC 20091.

AARP Foundation. HUD/HECM Counselor Training Program (forthcoming). Call 202-434-6030 for availability. (video/workbook)

Scholen, Ken. Retirement Income On The House; Cashing In On Your Home With A "Reverse" Mortgage, NCHEC Press, Apple Valley, MN, 1994

Scholen, Ken. Your New Retirement Nest Egg: A Consumer Guide to the New Reverse Mortgages (second edition), NCHEC Press, Apple Valley, MN, 1996.

Scholen, Ken and Jerry Wagner. The Reverse Mortgage Counselor, Version 2.2, NCHEC, Apple Valley, MN, 1998. (software)

Federal Law

Code of Federal Regulations (CFR) Title 12 Banks and Banking; Part 226 Truth in Lending (Regulation Z); Section 226.33 - Requirements for Reverse Mortgages

Code of Federal Regulations (CFR) Title 12 Banks and Banking; Part 226 Truth in Lending (Regulation Z); Appendix K - Calculating TALC Rates for Reverse Mortgages

Code of Federal Regulations (CFR) Title 24 Housing and Urban Development; Part 206 - Home Equity Conversion Mortgage Insurance

12 U. S. Code 1715z-20. Demonstration program of insurance of home equity conversion mortgages

U. S. Department of Housing and Urban Development. Home Equity Conversion Mortgages: HUD Handbook 4235.1, Washington DC 1994

> Link from the "Bibliography" page at **www.reverse.org** directly into government websites where you can search for, view, and download the federal laws listed above.

Market Analysis

George, Linda K. "Economic Status and Well-Being: A Review of the Literature and an Agenda for Future Research," in Aging, Money, and Life Satisfaction, Springer, 1992.

Kutty, Nandinee. "The Scope for Poverty Alleviation among Elderly Homeowners in the United States through Reverse Mortgages," Cornell University, 1995.

Mayer, Christopher, and Katerina Simons. "Reverse Mortgages and the Liquidity of Housing Wealth," Journal of the American Real Estate and Urban Economics Association, Summer, 1994.

Merrill, Sally, Meryl Finkel, and Nandinee Kutty. "Potential Beneficiaries from Reverse Mortgage Products for the Elderly," AREUEA Journal, 1995, 22(2):257-99.

Rasmussen, David. "The Demand for Reverse Mortgages: A Survey of Elderly Homeowners," Florida State University, 1995.

Rasmussen, David, Isaac Megbolugbe, and Barbara Morgan. "Reverse Mortgages: Private Incentives, Market Constraints, and Public Policy," Fannie Mae, 1995.

Rasmussen, David, Isaac Megbolugbe, and Barbara Morgan. "Using the 1990 Public Use Microdata Sample to Estimate Potential Demand for Reverse Mortgage Products," Journal of Housing Research, Vol.. 6, Issue 1, 1995.

U. S. Department of Housing and Urban Development. Evaluation of the Home Equity Conversion Mortgage Insurance Demonstration, Washington, DC, 1995

Link from the "Bibliography" page at **www.reverse.org** directly into the HUD User website, where you can order online for $5.00 the HECM evaluation listed at the bottom of the previous page.

Program Design

Guttentag, Jack. "Creating New Financial Instruments for the Aged," New York University, Graduate School of Business Administration, Center for the Study of Financial Institutions, 1975.

Phillips, William and Stephen Gwin. "Reverse Mortgages," Transactions (Vol. XLIV), Society of Actuaries, Schaumburg, IL, 1993

Scholen, Ken. "Consumer Response to Reverse Mortgage: A Blueprint for Product Development," National Center for Home Equity Conversion, 1993.

Scholen, Ken. "Final Report of the Home Equity Conversion Project," State of Wisconsin, Bureau on Aging, 1982.

Scholen, Ken. Marketing Reverse Mortgages: Keys to Market Growth, NCHEC, 1996.

Scholen, Ken and Yung-Ping Chen (eds.). Unlocking Home Equity for the Elderly, Ballinger Publishing, Cambridge, MA, 1981.

Szymanoski, Jr., Edward J. The FHA Home Equity Conversion Mortgage Insurance Demonstration: A Model to Calculate Borrower Payments and Insurance Risk, U. S. Department of Housing and Urban Development, Washington, DC, 1990

Szymanoski, Jr., Edward J. "Risk and the Home Equity Conversion Mortgage," AREUEA Journal, 1994, 22(2):347-99.

U. S. Department of Housing and Urban Development. Home Equity Conversion Mortgages: HUD Handbook 4235.1, Washington DC 1994

Link from the "Bibliography" page at **www.reverse.org** directly into the HUD Library, where you can search for, view, and download the HUD/HECM Handbook (4235.1).

Program Evaluation

U. S. Department of Housing and Urban Development. Evaluation of the Home Equity Conversion Mortgage Insurance Demonstration, Washington, DC, 1995

Link from the "Bibliography" page at **www.reverse.org** directly into the HUD User website, where you can order online for $5.00 the comprehensive HECM evaluation listed above.

Public Policy

Jacobs, Bruce, and William Weissert. "Using Home Equity to Finance Long-Term Care," Journal of Health Politics, Policy and Law, Spring, 1987.

Redfoot, Donald L. "Long-Term Care Reform and the Role of Housing Finance," Housing Policy Debate, Vol. 4, 1993.

Redfoot, Donald L. "The Role of Housing Finance in Long Term Care Reform," Lusk Review, 1996.

Scholen, Ken (ed.). Model State Law on Reverse Mortgages, AARP Foundation, 1997.

Scholen, Ken. "An Analysis of the HUD Report on Reverse Mortgage Insurance," AARP Federal Affairs, 1986.

Scholen, Ken. "Financing Home Care with Home Equity," Journal of Long Term Home Health Care, 1983.

Scholen, Ken. "Home Equity Conversion in the United States: Programs, Data, and Potential Public Policy Issues," AARP Public Policy Institute, 1991.

Scholen, Ken. "Home-Made Health Care Financing," American Health Care Association Journal, August, 1982.

Scholen, Ken. "Reverse Mortgage Counseling: Preparing for the Next Stage of Market Development," AARP Consumer Affairs, 3/1/92.

Scholen, Ken. "Strengthening Cost Disclosures on Reverse Mortgages," NCHEC, Apple Valley, MN, 1998.

Scholen, Ken. "Taxing Self-Reliance: State Taxes on Reverse Mortgages," AARP Consumer Affairs, 1993.

Scholen, Ken. "Using Home Equity To Pay For Long Term Care," State of Connecticut Governor's Commission on Long Term Care Financing, 1987.

Scholen, Ken, Maurice Weinrobe, Bruce Jacobs, Jay Greenberg, and William Weissert. "The Role of Home Equity in Financing Long Term Care," Minnesota State Housing Finance Agency, 1986.

U. S. Department of Housing and Urban Development. "Home Equity Conversion Mechanisms," December, 1985, Washington, DC.

Chapter 11

The Market

Where did reverse mortgages come from? And who are the pioneering consumers who have been the first reverse mortgage borrowers?

This chapter provides some answers to these questions. It starts with a quick look at the current size and shape of the reverse mortgage market.

Size & Shape

Based on proprietary and public data it has collected, the National Center for Home Equity Conversion (NCHEC) estimates that the total number of **private sector** reverse mortgages ever closed in the United States through March of 1998 totaled about 45,000 loans.

- Over half of these loans have been federally insured Home Equity Conversion Mortgages.
- In the three decades from 1961 through 1990, only about 3,000 private sector reverse mortgages were closed.
- Then, over the next two years (1991-92), about another 5,000 were closed.
- About 80% of all reverse mortgages ever closed have been written in the past 5 years.

In addition to these private sector loans, state and local governments have made **public sector** reverse mortgages for specified purposes:

- paying property taxes or special assessments,
- repairing or improving homes,
- making home modifications to enhance independence.

In 1991, NCHEC estimated that the total number of such transactions was about 143,000.

Pioneering Consumers

An evaluation of the Home Equity Conversion Mortgage (HECM) program was published by the U. S. Department of Housing and Urban Development in March of 1995. The key findings were these:

- Median borrower age = 76 years.
- Median annual income of borrowers = $10,400 (44% less than the median income of all elderly homeowners).
- Median home value of borrowers = $102,000 (45% greater than the median value of homes owned by all elderly homeowners).
- 57% of all borrowers selected a line-of-credit only; another 24% selected a creditline plus a monthly advance.
- Six out of ten loans were made to females living alone.
- Three out of four borrowers reported having no children.
- 45% of the loans involved home values exceeding HUD's 203-b equity limits.
- Loan volume had tripled in two years.
- Loans had been closed in 46 states; nearly 50% were closed in 5 states: CA, NY, IL, CO, NJ.

A Capsule History

1961

- First reverse mortgage reverse mortgage loan made by Nelson Haynes of Deering Savings & Loan (Portland, ME) to Nellie Young, the widow of his high school football coach

1963

- First property tax deferral program offered in Oregon, financed through Public Employees Retirement Fund

1970

- Survey research on a "housing annuity plan" conducted in Los Angeles by Yung-Ping Chen of UCLA

1975

- Technical monograph on "Creating New Financial Instruments for the Aged" authored by Jack M. Guttentag of The Wharton School

1977

- First RM loan program, "Equi-Pay", introduced by Arlo Smith and Emma Linek of Broadview Savings & Loan in Independence, OH

1978

- "Reverse Mortgage Study Project" funded by Wisconsin Bureau on Aging, directed by Ken Scholen
- First statewide deferred payment loan program offered by WI Dept of Local Affairs and Development, designed by William Perkins

1979

- First national conference on reverse mortgages ("Reverse Mortgage Development Conference") sponsored by Wisconsin Bureau on Aging in Madison, WI on 5/21-22
- San Francisco Development Fund's "Reverse Annuity Mortgage (RAM)" program funded by Federal Home Loan Bank Board, foundations, and WI Bureau on Aging; directed by Don Ralya

1980

- **Unlocking Home Equity for the Elderly**, edited by Ken Scholen and Yung-Ping Chen, published by Ballinger (Cambridge, MA)
- Two-year "Home Equity Conversion Project" funded by U.S. Administration on Aging, directed by Ken Scholen
- FHA reverse mortgage insurance proposal by Ken Scholen endorsed by housing pre-conference to 1981 White House Conference on Aging

1981

- National Center for Home Equity Conversion (NCHEC) incorporated as independent, non-profit organization in Madison, WI; directed by Ken Scholen
- U. S. House Select Committee on Aging hears first Congressional testimony on reverse mortgages, by Ken Scholen
- White House Conference on Aging endorses proposal recommending that "the FHA should develop an insurance program for reverse mortgage loans"
- Newsweek, Time, U.S. News, Good Morning America provide first national media exposure for reverse mortgages
- San Francisco RAM program closes first loans

1982

- "National Potential for Home Equity Conversion" authored by Bruce Jacobs (University of Rochester)
- San Francisco RAM program expands to new sites in California, directed by Bronwyn Belling
- U. S. Administration on Aging funds NCHEC research on federal issues - including FHA reverse mortgage insurance
- U. S. Senate Special Committee on Aging stages first hearing on reverse mortgages; staffed by

John Rother; testimony by Ken Scholen, Jack Guttentag, Maurice Weinrobe, James Firman

- U. S. Senate Special Committee on Aging issues report citing need for reverse mortgage insurance
- Garn-St. Germain Depository Institutions Act clears regulatory path for reverse mortgages; first federal statutory recognition

1983

- Federal Council on Aging supports proposal for FHA reverse mortgage insurance
- FHA reverse mortgage insurance demonstration program proposed by U.S. Department of Housing and Urban Development (HUD) in housing bill
- "Reverse Mortgages: Problems and Prospects for a Secondary Market and an Examination of Mortgage Guaranty Insurance", authored by Maurice Weinrobe (Clark University)
- "National Development Conference" sponsored by NCHEC with HUD support in Washington, DC; greetings sent by President Ronald Reagan and U. S. Representative Claude Pepper
- U.S. Administration on Aging funds NCHEC information and training project
- "Home Equity Financing of Long-Term Care for the Elderly" authored by Bruce Jacobs (University of Rochester) and William Weissert (Urban Institute)

- FHA insurance proposal by Sen. John Heinz adopted by Senate; House-Senate conference committee mandates HUD study

1984

- First open-ended, risk-pooling reverse mortgage offered by American Homestead in New Jersey
- RAM program and NCHEC provide training and technical assistance to new reverse mortgage programs in AZ, MA, NY, and WI
- Prudential-Bache announces marketing agreement with American Homestead
- Social Security Administration releases policy memo on treatment of income from HEC plans

1985

- HUD sponsors conference on home equity conversion
- U. S. Senate and House Aging Committees sponsor joint briefing session for Congressional staffers, moderated by Ken Scholen
- Line-of-credit reverse mortgage development project initiated by United Seniors Health Cooperative (DC), directed by Bronwyn Belling
- First "split-term" reverse mortgage offered by CT Housing Finance Agency, designed by Stuart Jennings and Arnold Pritchard

1986

- "Home Equity Information Center" established by AARP, directed by Katrinka Smith Sloan
- American Homestead expands into CT, OH, and PA
- California Home Equity Conversion Coalition established by RAM program counselors
- MA Elderly Equity Program funded by Commonwealth of Massachusetts, directed by Len Raymond
- HUD releases study opposing a federal reverse mortgage insurance demonstration
- AARP releases analysis by Ken Scholen critiquing HUD study; AARP urges enactment of federal RM insurance demonstration

1987

- NCHEC completes studies on home equity financing of long-term care for Minnesota and Connecticut
- U.S. House Ways and Means Committee hears testimony on RM and long-term care by James Firman (United Seniors) and Ken Scholen (NCHEC)
- Congress passes FHA reverse mortgage insurance proposal
- American Homestead expands into DE, MD, & VA

- "Home-Made Money: A Consumer Guide to HEC" published by AARP, authored by Ken Scholen

1988

- National survey of members' reverse mortgage needs and preferences by AARP
- FHA reverse mortgage insurance legislation signed by President Reagan on 2/5/88; Judith V. May named by HUD to develop program
- "Innovation in Hone Equity Conversion" conference sponsored by AARP; attracts 200 participants from 25 states
- New plan announced by Capital Holding Corporation (Louisville, KY); 10th largest investor-owned insurance company in America: "Home Income Security Plan" first offered in KY, MD, and VA
- First line-of-credit reverse mortgage developed by VA Housing Development Authority
- American Homestead expands into CA
- Providential Home Income Plan (San Francisco) offers shared-appreciation plan in CA
- HUD releases proposed regulations for FHA reverse mortgage insurance program
- Fannie Mae announces intention to purchase reverse mortgages insured by FHA

- U. S. Administration on Aging announces cooperative agreement with HUD to sponsor training of reverse mortgage counselors

1989

- "A Financial Guide to Reverse Mortgages" authored by Ken Scholen for NCHEC; introduces total loan cost rate method for analyzing costs
- HUD selects 50 lenders by lottery to make first FHA-insured reverse mortgages
- Software for determining reverse mortgage loan advances developed by FHA and made available to the public
- Wendover Funding (NC) announces program for servicing FHA-insured reverse mortgages
- HUD releases "Home Equity Conversion Mortgage" (HECM) program handbook (# 4235.1)
- Fourteen 2-day counselor training sessions conducted by Bronwyn Belling (AARP) and Ken Scholen (NCHEC) for FHA
- Capital Holding expands into CA and FL
- FNMA announces policies for purchasing FHA-insured (HECM) reverse mortgages
- First FHA-insured HECM made to Marjorie Mason of Fairway, KS by the James B Nutter Co
- National Center for Home Equity Conversion (NCHEC) moves from Madison, WI to Marshall, MN

1990

- AARP releases FHA Counselor Training and Reference Manual, by Bronwyn Belling and Ken Scholen
- American Homestead and Providential suspend lending as recession and falling appreciation expectations dry up debt sources for new loans
- Fourteen more 2-day counselor training sessions conducted by Bronwyn Belling (AARP) and Ken Scholen (NCHEC) for HUD
- "Reverse Angle" newsletter published for FHA counselors by AARP Home Equity Information Center
- Congress increases FHA insurance authority to 25,000 loans by 9/31/95; requires disclosure of total loan cost and development of equity reserve option
- AARP publishes "Model State Law on Reverse Mortgages"
- HUD publishes "FHA Home Equity Conversion Insurance Demonstration: A Model to Calculate Borrower Payments and Insurance Risk," by Edward Szymanoski Jr.

1991

- Los Angeles County Employees Retirement Association sponsors information seminar on reverse mortgages as a potential fund investment and member benefit

- AARP publishes 3rd edition of "Home-Made Money" by Ken Scholen; distribution tops 250,000
- New consumer guide developed by Federal Trade Commission in partnership with NCHEC and AARP
- HUD publishes new regulations making reverse mortgage insurance available to all FHA lenders
- Interim report on FHA program by Judith V. May
- **Retirement Income On The House: Cashing In On Your Home With A "Reverse" Mortgage**, 352-page book by Ken Scholen with a preface by Jane Bryant Quinn published by NCHEC
- National Leadership Conference on Home Equity Conversion sponsored by AARP (9/91)
- First lifetime reverse mortgage programs proposed by Peter Mazonas of HomeFirst (San Francisco) and Robert Bachman of Home Equity Partners (Irvine, CA)
- FNMA expands funding for expanded HECM program; develops comprehensive "Instruction Package"
- Wendover Funding announces correspondent program and "starter kit" for lenders
- First multi-state HECM lending programs developed by International Mortgage (DE, DC, MD, PA, VA, WV), Directors Mortgage (AZ, CA, NV), and ARCS Mortgage (CA, HI, NY, OR, WA)

1992

- Capital Holding Corporation airs 60-second and 120-second prime-time network television ads in CA and FL for its "Homearnings" plan
- Initial public stock offering by Providential Home Income Plan attracts strong investor interest
- AARP publishes 79-page discussion paper on reverse mortgage counseling by Ken Scholen
- AARP releases videotape for counselor training written and narrated by Ken Scholen
- U. S. Securities & Exchange Commission issues directive prohibiting interest accrual in reverse mortgage accounting
- U. S. Securities & Exchange Commission rescinds previous directive; issues directive on effective yield method for reverse mortgage accounting
- AARP sponsors community coalition-building seminars in support of HECM program development in OH, WI, IA, NY, NJ, PA, IL
- **Retirement Income On The House: Cashing In On Your Home With A "Reverse" Mortgage** named best book of 1992 on financial services for the elderly by the National Association of State Units on Aging (NASUA)
- HECM preliminary evaluation released by HUD

1993

- Transamerica announces reverse mortgage product including deferred annuity from MetLife
- Fannie Mae convenes roundtable on conventional reverse mortgages
- Capital Holding discontinues "Homearnings" plan
- NCHEC prepares report on state taxation of reverse mortgage transactions for AARP
- Home Equity Partners (Irvine, CA) and Union Labor Life announce new "Freedom" plan including immediate annuity from MetLife
- Wendover Funding convenes 2-day conference of HECM originators
- AARP sponsors community seminars in support of HECM program development in CA, LA, MI, and MS
- Fannie Mae initiates series of information sessions for financial planners and elderlaw attorneys
- Andrus Gerontology Center (USC) convenes national teleconference on reverse mortgages
- National Center for Home Equity Conversion moves from Marshall, MN to Apple Valley, MN
- At year's end, the HECM program is all states except AK, SD, and TX); Unity Mortgage offers it in 25 states; Senior Income in 14 states; Directors Mortgage in 14 states; Amerifirst Mortgage in 9 states; ARCS Mortgage in 6 states; International Mortgage in 4 states

1994

- Household Senior Services offers "Ever Yours" creditline reverse mortgage in FL, GA, IL, KY, MD, MI, OH, and VA
- Congress enacts "total loan cost rate" disclosure requirement for all reverse mortgages; Federal Reserve publishes proposed regulations
- NCHEC prepares report on "Reversing Foreclosures" for AARP
- New York rescinds mortgage tax on reverse mortgages
- U. S. Court of Appeals (5th Circuit; # 93-8170; First Gibralter V. Morales) removes legal barrier to RM lending in Texas; Rep. Gonzales legislates statutory override of court decision
- CA Public Employees Retirement System (CALPERS) initiates study of reverse mortgage investment
- Transamerica HomeFirst introduces creditline plan and expands into NY, NJ, PA, and CT
- At year's end, Unity Mortgage is offering the FHA/HECM plan in 42 states and Director's Mortgage has merged with Norwest Bank

1995

- HUD releases "Evaluation of the Home Equity Conversion Mortgage Insurance Demonstration"

- HUD releases first major revision of HECM handbook (#4235.1 REV-1)
- HUD approves direct endorsement processing of HECM loans
- NCHEC publishes **Your New Retirement Nest Egg: A Consumer Guide to the New Reverse Mortgages** by Ken Scholen, 336 pages
- AARP publishes 5th edition of "Home-Made Money" by Ken Scholen; distribution tops 400,000
- HECM program lapses at end of federal fiscal year
- AARP sponsors national conference on reverse mortgages in MD on 11/14-15
- Fannie Mae announces "HomeKeeper" reverse mortgage; coverage includes front-page, above-the-fold article in USA Today
- FHA Commissioner's Award presented by Nicolas Retsinas to Ken Scholen for his work on reverse mortgages

1996

- HECM program re-authorized on January 26, 1996
- Fannie Mae begins lender training for "Home Keeper"
- NCHEC issues Second Edition of **Your New Retirement Nest Egg: A Consumer Guide to the New Reverse Mortgages** by Ken Scholen, 352 pp.

- Hartford Life tests annuity complement to HECM and Fannie Mae reverse mortgages
- HUD initiates counselor training via satellite TV

1997

- AARP releases consumer videotapes written by Ken Scholen featuring Scholen and Bronwyn Belling
- AARP sponsors HUD counselor training via satellite TV featuring Belling and Scholen
- Referral fee scams denounced by AARP, HUD, Fannie Mae
- Household Senior Services discontinues "Forever Yours" plan
- AARP announces counselor support fund capitalized by HUD and Fannie Mae
- NCHEC initiates "preferred" lender and counselor program and releases "Reverse Mortgage Counselor" software
- Ibis Software (SF) releases "Reverse Mortgage Originator" software
- Texas approves referendum intended to permit reverse mortgages, but technical errors make impact uncertain, problematic
- AARP sponsors national reverse mortgage leadership roundtable and conference

- National Reverse Mortgage Lenders Association (NRMLA) organized by Jeffrey Taylor with Peter Bell as staff
- NCHEC launches exploratory project on public sector incentives for home equity financing of long term care

1998

- NCHEC circulates discussion paper on "Strengthening Cost Disclosures on Reverse Mortgages" by Ken Scholen
- AARP releases "HECM Training-in-a-Box" including videotapes, workbook, HECM handbook, and counseling manual
- Fannie Mae conducts research to identify reverse mortgage market segments
- NCHEC publishes "Reverse Mortgages for Beginners: A Consumer Guide to Every Homeowner's Retirement Nest Egg," 132 pages
- NCHEC establishes website at **www.reverse.org**

Glossary

adjustable rate - an interest rate that changes based on changes in a published market rate index

annuity – a monthly cash advance for life from an insurance company (i. e., as used in this book, a "defined benefit, fixed" annuity)

appreciation - an increase in the value of a home

appraisal - an estimate of a home's market value

bubble (see cost bubble)

capital gains tax - a tax on increases in home value

closing - a meeting at which legal documents are signed to "close the deal" on a mortgage; the time at which a mortgage begins

cost bubble - a sharp increase in the Total Annual Loan Cost on a reverse mortgage

creditline - a credit account that permits a borrower to control the timing and amount of the loan advances; also known as a "line-of-credit"

default - the failure of a borrower or lender to fulfill agreed-upon mortgage terms

deferred payment loans - reverse mortgages providing lump sums for repairing or improving homes

depreciation - a decrease in the value of a home

equity conservation - a feature permitting borrowers to pre-select their debt limit

Fannie Mae - a private company that buys and sells mortgages; a government-sponsored entity (GSE) that operates under the general oversight of the federal government; also known as the Federal National Mortgage Association (FNMA)

fixed-term - a reverse mortgage that becomes due and payable on a specific date

home equity - the value of a home minus any debt against it

home equity conversion - turning home equity into cash without having to leave your home or make regular loan repayments

Home Equity Conversion Mortgage (HECM) - the only reverse mortgage program insured by the Federal Housing Administration (FHA), which is part of the U. S. Department of Housing and Urban Development (HUD)

HomeKeeper - the reverse mortgage program developed and backed by Fannie Mae

joint tenancy - equal ownership rights held by two or more persons that survive the death of any owner

lifetime advances - fixed monthly loan advances for the rest of a borrower's life

leftover equity - net sale proceeds minus total amount owed

loan advances - payments made to a borrower, or to another party on behalf of a borrower

loan balance - the amount owed, including principal and interest; limited in a reverse mortgage by a non-recourse feature

loan term - the period of time from closing until the loan is due and payable

lump sum - a single loan advance at closing

maturity - when a loan becomes due and payable

mortgage - a legal document making a home available to a lender to satisfy a debt

National Center for Home Equity Conversion (NCHEC) - an independent nonprofit national organization specializing exclusively in reverse mortgage education and analysis since 1981

non-recourse mortgage - a loan in which a lender may only look to the value of the home for repayment

origination - the administrative process of setting up a mortgage, including the preparation of documents

percent of value pricing - basing the total amount owed on a percent of a home's value at maturity

principal - see loan advances

property tax deferrals - reverse mortgages providing annual loan advances for paying property taxes

reverse annuity mortgage - a reverse mortgage in which a lump sum is used to purchase an annuity

reverse mortgage - a non-recourse loan against home equity providing cash advances to a borrower and requiring no repayment until a future time

servicing - performing administrative functions on a loan after closing

shared appreciation - an itemized loan cost based on a percent of any increase in the value of a home

shared equity - an itemized loan cost based on a percent of a home's value at loan maturity

Supplemental Security Income (SSI) - a federal program providing monthly cash benefits to low-income persons aged 65+, blind, or disabled

tenure advances - fixed monthly loan advances for as long as a borrower lives in a home

term advances - fixed monthly loan advances for a specific period of time

Total Annual Loan Cost (TALC) rate - the projected annual average cost of a reverse mortgage including all costs as limited by the non-recourse feature

Acknowledgements

Nobel Prize in Economics Laureate Paul A. Samuelson in a foreword to the first book on on reverse mortgages in 1980 wrote

> We sing the praises of inventors in science who give us better consumer goods. We honor life scientists who help us live more years of happy health. And this is proper. But we should also voice our thanks to innovators of new social mechanisms that can add to human happiness. I applaud the present research and experiments on home equity conversion.

In two decades of involvement with reverse mortgages, I have seen the essential role played by "social mechanism scientists" – the creative technicians who analyze the options, tinker with the variables, and make the design breakthroughs. Over the past decade in particular, it's been my good fortune to have worked with – and learned from - several of them.

Ed Szymanoski, Jr. was the chief technician on the team that developed the HECM program. That product's flexibility - including its growing creditline - has never been matched. Ed's 1990 paper on reverse mortgage risk is still the most in-depth treatment you will find. Best of all, his expertise and dedication are still serving the public at HUD's Division of Policy Development and Research.

The Office of the Comptroller of the Currency had the good sense to snatch Nick Kiritz away from Fannie Mae last year. But not before he'd completed his stellar work on Fannie's groundbreaking Home-Keeper plan. A long-needed complement to HECM, this plan's unique structural features have made a major contribution to the reverse mortgage market.

James Brown may or may not be "the hardest working man in show business." But Jerry Wagner of Ibis Capital clearly takes the toil and productivity cake in reverse mortgages. He's also the sharpest analytical mind we've seen in this market.

Jerry's pioneering work on product comparison software has made it possible for consumers to understand their choices fully before making a decision. His breakthrough design efforts produced the first reverse annuity mortgage providing sound options for a wide range of homeowners. And along the way his pedagogical skills have raised the level of technical literacy throughout the reverse mortgage market.

Wynton Marsalis has opined that greater technical proficiency can lead to greater artistry and creativity. The technical expertise of Ed, Nick, and Jerry clearly has allowed them to imagine and create elegant design solutions to problems that others could not even see. And for that we are the richer. Moreover, the broader sense of social dedication and responsibility so evident in their work has exemplified what is still so attractive and compelling about this market.

Ken Scholen
Apple Valley, Minnesota March 6, 1998

About NCHEC

The National Center for Home Equity Conversion (NCHEC) is an independent, nonprofit organization established in 1981 to educate consumers about reverse mortgages. It grew out of the first reverse mortgage research projects sponsored by the United States Administration on Aging.

The Center has provided leadership for conferences and training sessions in 46 states, and has assisted reverse mortgage development in Argentina, Australia, Canada, Japan, England, and Spain. NCHEC advocates for sound consumer products and business practices, but endorses no specific reverse mortgage products.

The Center received startup grants from the Retirement Research Foundation (Chicago), the Florence V. Burden Foundation (New York), and the Kimberly Clark Foundation (Wisconsin). Since then it has been supported principally by research and training grants, consulting for consumer organizations, and sales of its consumer education materials.

NCHEC was initially located in Madison, WI, moved to Marshall, MN in 1989, and to its present location in 1993.

National Center for Home Equity Conversion
7373 147 Street #115
Apple Valley, MN 55124
612-953-4474; 612-953-3230 (fax)
www.reverse.org

About the Author

NCHEC founder and director Ken Scholen has specialized in reverse mortgage analysis and education since 1978. He has written critically-acclaimed consumer guides, counseling software, developed NCHEC's website, and has trained over 5,000 consumer counselors, government officials, professional advisors, and mortgage personnel. He has been AARP's principal consultant on reverse mortgages since 1986.

Scholen first proposed federal reverse mortgage insurance in 1980, assisted in drafting the HECM statute, and helped HUD design the program. He developed the total loan cost analysis adopted by Congress in amending Truth-in-Lending laws, and advocated the reverse mortgage accounting methods adopted by the U.S. Securities & Exchange Commission. In 1995, he received the Federal Housing Commissioner's Award for his work in the field.

Scholen has been a studio guest on CNBC and "Good Morning America," has appeared on the NBC Nightly News, and has been a featured speaker at AARP's Biennial Convention.

In other areas, Scholen has directed a state board on aging, co-founded a statewide senior advocacy coalition, developed an innovative senior housing facility, directed a comprehensive senior services organization, conducted research in city government, and lobbied for six years on child welfare issues. He was a founding board member of United Seniors Health Cooperative (DC) and the Wisconsin Partnership for Housing Development.